100+ IDEAS
FOR SUPPORTING
CHILDREN WITH DYSLEXIA

CONTINUUM ONE HUNDREDS SERIES

100 Ideas for Supporting Pupils with ADHD, Geoff Kewley and
Pauline Latham

100 Ideas for Supporting Pupils with Dyspraxia and DCD,
Amanda Kirby and Lynne Peters

*100 Ideas for Supporting Pupils with Social, Emotional and
Behavioural Difficulties*, Roy Howarth

Also Available from Continuum

Dyslexia 3rd Edition, Gavin Reid

Effective Learning, Gavin Reid and Shannon Green

Teaching Assistant's Guide to Dyslexia, Gavin Reid and
Shannon Green

100+ IDEAS
FOR SUPPORTING CHILDREN WITH DYSLEXIA

Gavin Reid and Shannon Green

Continuum One Hundreds

continuum

Continuum International Publishing Group

The Tower Building   80 Maiden Lane
11 York Road   Suite 704, New York
London, SE1 7NX   NY 10038

www.continuumbooks.com

British Library Cataloguing-in-Publication Data
A catalogue record for this book is available from the British
Library.

ISBN: 978-0-8264-3416-6 (paperback)

Library of Congress Cataloging-in-Publication Data
Reid, Gavin.
100+ ideas for supporting children with dyslexia / Gavin Reid
and Shannon Green. p. cm. Includes bibliographical
references.
ISBN 978–0-8264–3416–6 – ISBN 978–1-4411–7406-2 –
ISBN 978–1-4411–3093-8 1. Dyslexic children–Education.
2. Reading disability. I. Green, Shannon. II. Title. III. Title:
One hundred plus ideas for supporting children with dyslexia.

LB1050.5.R446 2011
371.91'44–dc22   2011000384

Typeset by Newgen Imaging System Pvt, Ltd, Chennai, India
Printed and bound in India

CONTENTS

SECTION 3 **Differentiation**

SECTION 4 **Planning for learning**

SECTION 5 **Learning strategies**

SECTION 8 Creative writing

Dyslexia can be a confusing condition. There are plenty of theories on the nature of dyslexia from visual deficit and dietary imbalance theories to speculation on movement and coordination difficulties. We understand that the busy teacher often does not have time to read the latest literature and generate new teaching approaches. So, the concept behind this book is to provide a range of ready-made ideas which have been tried and tested and are effective in helping to support students with dyslexia in the classroom. The ideas in this book can all be easily modified by teachers for their own particular classroom and school context, and are relevant to teachers from all sectors at primary and secondary level (ages 5–19).

Early identification and knowledge of the characteristics of dyslexia are important and so we have introduced many of the ideas with some commentary. It is our aim that this book should inform as well as equip the teacher with some ready-made solutions.

Although there are a number of characteristics that can be associated with dyslexia; such as difficulties in reading accuracy, fluency, spelling, writing, organizing information, memorizing information and processing speed difficulties, the response to these difficulties lies firmly in the hands of the teacher and the school. Dyslexia relates a great deal to the learning context. In some schools the learning experience has been developed in a dyslexia-friendly manner in terms of the expectations, tasks that are set, materials available and how the information is presented. This can do much to reduce the impact of dyslexia on the individual.

We recognize that there is no one way of teaching students with dyslexia but by providing ideas we can stimulate and support the teacher to select and adapt accordingly. The ideas are all ready to use and do not need any special equipment. We hope that they are both time saving and informative and will help teachers become more confident and more skilled in dealing with dyslexia in the classroom.

In this second edition we have divided the book into eleven sections and rearranged the order of the sections to enhance clarity. We have developed twenty new ideas, extended many of the ideas in the first edition and added a glossary at the end of the book.

Dyslexia is a whole-school responsibility and not the responsibility of one teacher. The school management has a role to play in ensuring that cross-curricular initiatives in dyslexia are in place and that all teachers in both primary and secondary, including subject specialists, have some knowledge of dyslexia. Although most of the ideas in the book apply across the full range of subjects we have also included some subject-specific ideas in Section 11 relating to English, science, modern languages and music. In addition we have extended the section in mathematics. We have also added a new section (Section 3) on Differentiation – a practice that needs to be considered by all teachers to ensure that the materials, presentation and the assessment are all dyslexia friendly.

It is our hope you will find this second edition helpful and accessible, that it will inform your practice and be time saving in providing ready-made and appropriate responses to the challenges presented by children with dyslexia. The real beneficiaries of the ideas will be the children with dyslexia themselves. It is hoped that these ideas will lead to successful outcomes and the accompanying increase in self-esteem that is necessary if young people with dyslexia are to advance in education and society and fulfil their, often considerable, potential.

For the sake of simplicity, we have referred to the pupil as 'he' or 'him' throughout the book.

Gavin Reid and Shannon Green
January 2011

Teaching children with dyslexia – getting it right

Try to avoid having dyslexic pupils copy information from the board. It will take them a long time and they may have to stay behind to finish. This will make them feel different from others and as if they are failing in some way. It is also very likely that they will copy the information inaccurately. If it is essential to copy from the board it is best to use different colours of chalk or pen for each line. It is also an idea to pair a dyslexic pupil with a partner.

Try to provide the class with a choice – copy from the board or make notes from printed handouts. It is especially important that homework exercises are provided and given to dyslexic pupils in printed form.

Instead of writing on the board, type out the same notes and information and give these to the dyslexic pupil. Ask him to underline or highlight in colour the key points in these notes – remember to check that he has indicated the most appropriate key points. If he has difficulty in identifying these, give him two or three of them – perhaps at the beginning, middle and end of the notes – and ask him to fill in the rest. This exercise can be differentiated more by asking the pupil to identify a key point for each paragraph or for each sentence. If he does not have to copy notes from the board, more time will be available for this type of activity.

Alternatives to copying from the board

BOARD

✓ Provide notes

✓ Have another student copy their notes

✓ Highlight notes in colour

✓ Make own notes from key points

✓ Groups make up their own notes

Spellcheckers can be very useful but they do not always come up with the correct spelling as the dyslexic pupil's spelling pattern may be quite individual. The pupil may not know if the response from the spellchecker is actually correct. For example, if he writes 'to' instead of 'two' the spellchecker will show that as correct, even though it is not.

TextHelp is a particularly good spellchecking program for dyslexic pupils. This has a read-back facility and includes a spellcheck option that searches for common dyslexic errors. In addition, there is a word prediction feature that can predict a word from the context of the sentence and give up to ten options from a drop-down menu. Often dyslexic pupils have a word-finding difficulty and this feature can therefore be very useful. The software also has a 'word wizard' that provides the user with a definition of any word; an outline of a phonic map and a talking help file.

It's worth checking that the dyslexic pupil is able to use the spellchecker appropriately. Make a list of words he usually misspells. Put these into a personal spelling notebook for him. He should then put the meaning of the word next to it. This should include words that sound the same but have different spellings, such as 'night' and 'knight'. The pupil then checks the spelling alternatives from the spellchecker against his own personal spelling list.

OVERRELIANCE ON SPELLCHECKERS

COLOUR-CODED TIMETABLE

Colour-coded timetables are particularly relevant for dyslexic pupils when they reach secondary school. Try to use a different colour for different subjects. It is important that teachers recognize that dyslexic pupils may have a poor sense of direction and can arrive late for classes. They may even turn up for the wrong class at the wrong time. This can be particularly evident when they have recently transferred to a large secondary school – in fact it can take them years to find their way around the school without getting lost. They should have several copies of the colour-coded timetable, and the form teacher should have one readily available too. Timetables can get lost easily so discuss with the pupil some possible places to keep it, for example, taped to the inside of his backpack or bag or put in a page protector at the beginning of his binder. It may also be beneficial – for all pupils, not just the dyslexic ones – to display a large colour-coded timetable in the classroom.

It is an idea to get the pupil to put some key direction indicators on the back of the timetable. This might include, for example, history class – first floor, above main door beside the two pillars. Try to get the pupil to come up with these direction indicators himself as this will be more meaningful and will help him to retain the information.

Avoid using red pen when marking a dyslexic pupil's work. It is likely that there will be several spelling errors and it can be very disheartening to have every wrong spelling scored in red.

Ideally, homework and class work should be marked more for the content than for the presentation and accuracy. It is also important to appreciate that there is little point in the pupil rewriting work correctly. This can be time consuming and is not helpful. It may be better if you write out the word correctly and the pupil can look at this and note the mistakes that were made. He can then write over the top of the corrected word and name the letters aloud. This is a multisensory activity and this is the most effective method of learning for pupils with dyslexia, because it is visual, auditory and kinaesthetic.

Giving feedback after correcting work is very important. Ideally, this should be done on a one-to-one basis and in a constructive manner. Start with a positive comment, then indicate how the work could be improved. Feedback should be specific and realistic. It should focus on content – the pupil knows spelling is problematic so it isn't necessary to draw constant attention to that issue.

MARKING AND CORRECTING WORK

PRESENTING WORK

Ensure that the dyslexic pupil is familiar with the use of word processors and tape recorders as these are better for presenting work. The pupil's own voice can be a good aid to memory and this also involves active learning.

There are some excellent word processing programs available to help dyslexic people use word processors more effectively – programs like *TextHelp*, which helps with spelling and document presentation, and *Inspiration*, which helps with identifying key points and presenting work in a sequential and relevant manner. Both can be suitable for younger dyslexic children, as well as those at secondary school or college.

Get the pupil to try presenting the information orally first. He should think about his audience. Who will they be? How much of the topic will they know already? Will they all have the same level of knowledge? The introduction should be an overview of the presentation. This should be followed by a description of the main body of the information – get the pupil to identify the key issues and suggest why these are important. Finally comes the conclusion or summing up – this should also reinforce the key issues.

If the pupil is giving a talk and slides are to be used he needs to prepare them in advance and make sure they can be read by the whole audience (a point size of 28 or above is helpful). Only key words or phrases should be included, and advise him to avoid too much technical detail. Colour should be used appropriately – ensuring that the text can be easily read.

Often pupils with dyslexia will receive extra time in examinations. It is important to help them practise using this effectively and efficiently.

Allow the dyslexic pupil extra time from an early age to complete work, before he starts undertaking examinations. It is important, however, to ensure that the learner does not fall behind the work of the class because of the extra time being allocated to him.

Get the pupil to practise using extra time to:

- plan the answer
- check the content of the answer
- check spelling and grammar.

It is best to tackle each of these aspects individually at first. This will give the pupil practice at using extra time for that particular skill, such as planning, writing or checking.

The checking part is important as dyslexic pupils will need to read for both meaning and for punctuation, spelling and grammar. They will need time to ask themselves what the question is asking and whether they have answered the question fully and to the best of their ability. This means they will have to read over their work at least twice and time needs to be allocated for this. It is also a good idea to allow a break for the student to get up, stretch and have a drink of water midway through the exam. It will help with their focus and concentration.

Time will also need to be devoted to discussion after the exam so the student can reassess how they are using the additional time. Using extra time efficiently can take a lot of practice and evaluation with an emphasis on planning and using strategies to check and recheck their work. If the planning of the answer is carried out appropriately then they will have already made good use of the extra time.

Dyslexic pupils often experience failure at an early age due to their difficulties with reading and writing. This can result in a loss of self-esteem, which can become a major obstacle. It can be difficult to restore a positive self-image, but attempts must be made to do this as early as possible before this loss of self-esteem becomes too entrenched.

Try this exercise with younger children. At least every day for around 15 minutes – perhaps at the end of the day – get a group of children to sit in a circle. Go round the circle and get each child to say something positive about the person on their right. Then pair the children and get them to tell each other one thing they have learnt, or done that day, and why it is important. This gets them to think about each other in a positive way and also gets them thinking about their work in a positive manner. There are many other similar types of activities, but this is good because it involves the whole class and doesn't single out the dyslexic child. It is also an opportunity for the children to receive positive feedback and be part of a group.

PREPARING FOR COMFORT CIRCLES ACTIVITIES
It is a good idea to prepare children for this type of activity by pre-activity discussion.

Encourage children to come up with their own comments by doing a brainstorming activity where the children provide examples of positive and negative things to say.

For example:

Positive things to say	Negative things to say
I like the drawing you did today.	Your drawing looked like a baby did it.
You made me laugh when you said	That was a stupid thing to say.
I liked the way you included me in	I don't like playing with you.
Your story was interesting/funny.	You are boring.

Pupils with dyslexia often spend a lot of time on the basic skills of decoding print. This can be disheartening for them as it can be at the expense of more advanced learning and thinking skills. It is important to appreciate that although they have a reading difficulty, dyslexic pupils can also have a high level of intelligence. Activities to stimulate their intelligence should be available to them.

Make a list of tasks that can stimulate intelligence. These can include discussing ideas and beliefs, creative thinking and reflection activities. Develop an extended worksheet focusing on these aspects. This might begin with fundamental questions such as:

- Why?
- How?
- Justify?
- Compare?
- Evaluate?

These questions can become tasks that help dyslexic pupils develop higher order thinking skills and also allow opportunities for expansion of ideas.

Provide time for thinking and reflection. Try to provoke a follow-up response by giving positive feedback, such as:

- 'Good thinking so far'
- 'Interesting thought, tell me more . . . '
- 'Why do you think so?'
- 'Good thought!'
- 'What else could we do or think here to explain the situation or to remember/understand?'

STIMULATING INTELLIGENCE/THINKING AND RETHINKING

CREATING A DYSLEXIA-FRIENDLY CLASSROOM

The classroom environment can have a significant impact on dyslexic pupils. They may be having difficulties with listening, hearing, looking, sitting still, concentrating, writing and locating things they need. If their classroom environment is not dyslexia friendly they will have difficulty succeeding.

Dyslexia-friendly classrooms should be:

- arranged so that during class lessons, the dyslexic pupil can sit near the front
- adapted so that, wherever possible, dyslexic pupils can sit alongside well-motivated pupils or a 'study buddy' who they can ask to clarify instructions for them
- organized so that there is little movement around the room, which is kept as quiet as possible for some type of activities. Dyslexic pupils may find background noise and visual movement distracting when they are attempting to concentrate on challenging work
- equipped with clearly marked and neatly arranged resources so that they can be found easily. A visual can be used instead of a written label
- equipped with table lamps so that the main lights do not need to be used all the time
- organized so that wall displays are large and spaced out, not crowded in small areas
- adequately lit with as much natural light as possible
- equipped with a water supply so that water is readily available.

It is informative to listen to what young people with dyslexia say about being dyslexic. This can give an insight into how they see themselves and how they feel about their education. This information can then be used when developing teaching and learning materials.

Do this activity with a group of dyslexic pupils. Put them into pairs and ask them to think aloud and say how they feel about the work they are doing, and how being dyslexic affects them when they are doing this work. You may get the following comments:

- 'Languages are hard because everybody has finished and I've just started.'
- 'School work is very difficult for me – even with support.'
- 'I like scoring work points, but unfortunately I don't get too many.'
- 'I like it when an older student helps me and she is dyslexic too.'
- 'Sometimes I feel frustrated.'
- 'I have a lot of anger inside me. The real trouble starts at secondary school – they are too big and there is too much pressure.'
- 'It helps because my mum is dyslexic and she understands how hard school is for me.'
- 'I feel okay being dyslexic because I have a faster brain than anyone else.'
- 'I never finish my written work and my spelling is always wrong, even when I am copying from a book.'
- 'I am good at art, but I would rather be good at writing because you write all the time in school.'
- 'ICT is hard because I have to look backwards and forwards from the computer to the worksheet. I lose my place all the time and it takes ages.'
- 'Sometimes I feel very confused.'
- 'I asked my mum "Am I dyslexic?" She said, "yes". I said "cool".'

Use each comment as a way of following up how the pupils are progressing in their work. From the information you should be able to work out what they find difficult and why, and the barriers that are preventing them from succeeding.

Emotional literacy relates to being aware of one's emotions and the feelings of others. Children who are emotionally literate are able to perceive and understand their own feelings as well as other people's feelings. This can have implications for children with dyslexia because of the challenges they face in school; they can be sensitive and vulnerable.

Emotional literacy, to have any significant impact on the education of children, has to be fully absorbed and fully included into a whole-school ethos. There are a number of different views on the criteria for developing emotional intelligence but some of the factors that need to be considered are as follows:

- Emotional awareness – that is of the self and of others.
- Empathy – the need to be able to consider other people's viewpoint and feelings.
- Social competence – emotional literacy is usually articulated in a social setting so it is important that children are exposed to social learning that considers the emotional aspect of developing social competence. Group work, if carefully constructed and monitored, can be an ideal platform for developing social competence.

An emotional literacy programme can also have a beneficial spin-off effect on preventing bullying, enhancing communication, developing motivation, reflective and thinking skills, as well as developing interpersonal skills.

Use a checklist such as the one below to audit how prepared your school is for the development of an emotional literacy programme.

1. Have (I) we considered individual learning styles in our development plans?
2. Do (I) we cater for thinking skills in the curriculum?

3. Do we promote school groups, lunch-time groups and after-school groups? Can we do more to promote these?
4. How do we raise the self-esteem of the students? Can we do more to achieve this?
5. How do we cater for students who are experiencing emotional difficulties?
6. How do we achieve student motivation at the classroom level and the school level?
7. Is there a whole-school policy on emotional literacy?
8. Is there evidence in the corridors, school handbook, wall displays and in the classrooms that the school is culture friendly and recognizes diversity?
9. Do we have circle time programmes and have these been evaluated?

These questions can help the school staff and management assess the preparedness of the school or the class for developing an emotional literacy programme.

Teaching strategies

SMALL STEPS

Children with dyslexia often have difficulty with short-term and working memory. This means that they struggle to hold more than one or two points in their head at one time. If the task and the instructions are too long and complex they will have difficulty in retaining all the relevant information. Tasks should therefore be broken down into small steps. The small steps should be clearly shown and placed into a sequence. This can help with organization as it provides a structured framework.

The activity below highlights these steps and sequence. It involves the pupil summarizing the main idea of a chapter, or a section of a book, which the class has recently read. The small steps provide a structure that can help the reader sequence the chapter. Ask the pupil to:

- write down the names of the main characters
- identify the country(ies) where the story takes place
- identify which part of the country – the area
- write down four words that are important for the story. For example, in a story about warfare the words may be 'war, jet fighters, parachutes, gunfire'
- describe one event that happened in the chapter – you could develop this to describe one event from the beginning, one from the middle and one from the end, making it easier for the child to sequence the details of the story
- write down why that event was important.

Breaking the task down in this way will help the dyslexic pupil to focus on the information that is required and to provide a more relevant and detailed response.

The structure provided by the steps can also help to minimize the possibility of the pupil digressing from the key points.

Pre-task or pre-topic discussion provides an indication of pupils' current knowledge of the task or the area and whether they have the concepts and understanding needed to complete the task. Do this to ensure the dyslexic pupil has the necessary framework for the topic. It is a good idea to develop in advance a number of pre-reading discussion points. For example, if your class is studying, or about to study, the Spanish Armada the following could be pre-task discussion points:

- The geographical location of Spain
- The importance of ports
- The materials the ships are made from
- The instruments used for navigation
- The importance of trade.

Ask the class to note the key points that they have found out from the pre-reading discussion and, importantly, to identify why they are key points. This can be a writing exercise before they start reading. It will help the text to become more meaningful for the dyslexic pupil – the sequence should be discussion first, then writing and then reading.

This process will help to identity some key facts and concepts, helping the dyslexic pupil to understand the topic more fully and providing some necessary background information.

Keep sentences short and vocabulary simple. For example, the teacher might say, 'The Spanish Armada was a powerful maritime force and other countries feared the speed of the ships and the skills of the sailors.' Although that is not necessarily a long sentence it may be too long for pupils with dyslexia. There are three concepts/ideas in this sentence – *the force of the armada, the speed of the ships* and *the skills of the sailors*. The sentence could therefore have been presented as follows:

> The Spanish Armada was a powerful maritime force.
> Most of the countries nearby feared the speed of the Armada ships.
> The sailors of the Spanish Armada were well trained and well equipped.

It is important that sentences such as those above are supported with visuals. The pupil may rely heavily on visuals for understanding the content and concepts, as they can make the task more accessible. Highlight the key words with colour or bold text and, where possible, pictures. So, for example, the above sentences can be made easier for dyslexic pupils by inserting pictures after each one.

The page of a worksheet should be organized in a visually appealing manner and it is important also to use a 'dyslexia-friendly' font. Comic Sans, Century Gothic and Times New Roman are all considered dyslexia-friendly fonts. Establish the pupil's preferences – for example:

Do you prefer to read in this font? (Times New Roman)
Do you prefer to read in this one? (Comic Sans)
Or do you prefer to read in this style? (Century Gothic)

When you are considering the page layout:

- do not crowd the page
- use larger type
- use visuals where necessary
- remember to space out the information, using the whole page if appropriate.
- use indents for headings, subheadings, text
- use a bold font or highlighting for headings and/or keypoints
- fold the paper so you create a fold line for the student to comeback to

Heading

Subheading

Text

-
-
-
-

It is important that pupils with dyslexia are provided with opportunities for self-assessment. This is a useful skill to develop as it means that the pupil understands most of what he is reading or working on.

Tasks should be structured in a way that pupils can check to ensure they are doing it correctly. This can be done with review tasks and recapping sentences periodically. A checklist at the end of the task can be useful as this can help the learner monitor his progress.

At the start of the task the checklist might ask:

- What is my goal?
- What do I want to accomplish?
- What do I need to know before starting the task?
- What resources do I need?
- What is my deadline?

Midway through the task the pupil can ask himself:

- How am I doing?
- Do I need other resources to complete the task?
- What else can I do to finish the task?

Self-assessment is important as this emphasizes that the pupil has understood the task.

Questions that should be encouraged at the end of the task include:

- Did I accomplish my goal?
- Was I efficient?
- What worked?
- What did not work?
- Why did it not work?
- What strategies can I use next time?

Worksheets can present problems for dyslexic learners so it can be helpful to develop a checklist to ensure that they are dyslexia friendly. This can be used as a proactive guide for the teacher at the initial stage of development of worksheets, or pupil workbooks, and also as a monitoring tool later. The checklist can also be used as a guide for teachers who have little experience of dyslexia, such as newly qualified teachers, as it can provide them with some suggestions for presenting work for dyslexic learners.

A checklist could include the following:

Worksheet checklist	Yes/No
Have small steps been used?	
Are the sentences short?	
Is the vocabulary easy to understand?	
Have visuals been used?	
Has large print been used?	
Is the font style appropriate?	
Has enough attention been given to presentation?	
Are there opportunities for self-monitoring and self-correction?	
Are the tasks within the child's comfort zone?	
Is there a variety of different types of tasks?	
Are there opportunities for group work as well as individual work?	

FRAMEWORK FOR TEACHING

Children with dyslexia can learn in a different way from other pupils. It is crucial that they are allowed to do this and that school staff are aware of some general guidelines that help to recognize these differences in learning.

Developing a framework for teaching dyslexic children is therefore an important staff development exercise.

The framework can be used as a general guide for all teachers in a school. It may also be useful for trainee teachers undergoing placement in a school who may not have much knowledge or experience of dyslexia.

- Use charts and diagrams to highlight the bigger picture of what is being taught.
- Use mime and gesture to help the kinaesthetic learner (the pupil who prefers to learn through active involvement and experience). For example, drama is a good type of kinaesthetic activity.
- Add pictures to text.
- Use colour to highlight key words.
- Label diagrams and charts.
- Use games to consolidate vocabulary, make packs of pocket-sized cards showing important words.
- Use different colours for different purposes.
- Combine listening and reading by providing text and tape.
- Use mind-maps and spidergrams.
- Present information in small amounts with frequent opportunities for repetition and revision.

Differentiation

One of the main ways of ensuring success for children with dyslexia is to provide a range of means whereby they can demonstrate their competence. This may not necessarily be through the written mode so it is important that other means of displaying competence should be provided. Following are some suggestions:

- Investigation in groups
- Role-playing
- Making posters
- Brainstorming
- Sentence completion
- Quiz and competitions
- Videoing
- Worksheet activities
- Drama and role-play
- Fieldwork and enquiring
- Oral presentations
- Self-assessment
- Learning in pairs
- Cartoons and comic strips
- Completing tables
- Tape recording
- Debating
- Computer work
- Drawing pictures
- Making crosswords
- Journal writing
- Songs and poems.

These activities are usually very good for dyslexic children as they involve active participation and they do not necessarily require vast amounts of reading. Just some key instruction may be all that is necessary to get them started. This is important because if the structure is lacking, children with dyslexia, irrespective of the extent of differentiation that has taken place, may still flounder.

For example, the differentiated structure for the task Journal Writing may include the following:

1. Provide examples of Journals – this can be differentiated from (i) basic information type entries to (ii) opinions and points of reflections.

Basic questions

- What – what was the event?
- When – when did it take place – time, date?
- Where – did it happen – try to be exact
- Description – what happened? Who else was involved? Write at least three short sentences describing what happened.

Opinion and reflection questions

- How did you feel during this?
- Looking back is there anything you might have done differently?
- Write an entry 'advice to me' and comment on the event you are describing and how it had an influence on you, if any. Try to reflect on what you have learnt from the event.

2. Complete one entry in your journal and then decide how you can illustrate it. You can make smiley faces for good things and scowling faces for not so good points.
3. Design a cover for your journal.
4. Now you may want to think of a name for your journal – you can make it the same as the first entry or a more general title to reflect your overall activities.
5. Go to the library and look at some autobiographies. Look at some of the titles of these. You will notice they are usually 'eye-catching'. Try to think of a title for your journal – some ideas use one of the lines from a journal entry – for example, 'my bike is broken'; you can make it quite obscure as that will raise the reader's attention. Now you are ready for your journal!

DIFFERENTIATION BY CONTENT

It is important to try to ensure that the learning outcomes are the same for all. For example, the learning outcome for biology may be to describe all the features of a frog but the **content** of the activity sheet can be at different levels in terms of the ideas, concepts, use of visuals and vocabulary. The difference is that the route they take and the activities undertaken may be different to get to the same end. The task (how) and the content of the task (what) both need to be differentiated for students with dyslexia. When looking at the content you need to consider the following:

> **The text:** it is important to consider points such as vocabulary, length of sentences, clarity of phrases used, how the content builds on previous knowledge, the structure and style of the text, the avoidance of ambiguous sentences.
>
> **The use of visuals:** this can help to clarify the content and as a general rule more visuals should make the content simpler and clearer for learners with dyslexia.
>
> **The concepts:** it is important that the ideas and the concepts contained in the text are accessible.
>
> **Knowledge base:** it is best if you know the student's previous knowledge and understanding. Start with a recapping paragraph identifying the key points and stating why these are key points.

Following is an example of a description of what a frog is showing different types of activities at three different levels of differentiation. Each level has different demands but the overall learning outcomes can be accessed by all.

LEVEL 1 (DIFFICULT)

The frog has relatively smooth skin which varies in colour from olive green and yellow, to dark brown. It can also be speckled with black, brown or red and can lighten or darken to blend in with the surroundings.

The frog: *show a picture of a frog*
Skin: *smooth skin*
Colour: *olive green, yellow and dark brown*
Camouflage: *speckled and can lighten or darken
depending on surroundings.*

LEVEL 3 (THE MOST ACCESSIBLE FOR LEARNERS WITH DYSLEXIA)

The frog: show a number of pictures of a frog from different angles.

Annotation: highlight an annotated diagram of a frog showing clearly the different parts of the frog. This should be a large diagram so the text is clear and not too small.

Key words: this should be provided for the student so that he will be able to identify the key elements in the text.

What you need to find out and how: this should provide a structure for the student and provide an opportunity for self-checking to ensure that the student has achieved all the tasks. You could provide a self-checklist with all the tasks identified.

DIFFERENTIATION BY TASK

The task needs to be relevant and at the right conceptual level for the student but it must also be presented in a way that is accessible. Differentiation by task essentially involves ensuring the level and the means of presentation of the information is appropriate for the student. In order to do this you may have to identify the students learning preferences or ensure that the task can be accessed in a multisensory manner (visual, auditory and experiential learning). You should also try to incorporate investigative and metacognitive learning into the task. Investigative learning can be useful for students with dyslexia as it can develop their thinking skills. They may need some structure on how to carry out an investigation – even a checklist on what to do first, second, and so on can help.

Metacognitive learning is also useful as it helps the student take responsibility for his own learning. It can help the student reflect on what he has done and how he did it and importantly how he can develop this process the next time – for example, what he may want to do that he did not do this time.

Look at the headings below and reflect on how you can help students achieve them:

1. Self-questioning – knowing the right questions to ask yourself to make the task understandable and accessible.
2. Self-clarification – what other information will the student need to understand the task.
3. Self-understanding – confirmation that the student now understands the task.
4. Self-direction – ensuring that the student knows the next step to access the task.
5. Self-monitoring – ensuring that the student is able to monitor his own progress and is still focused on the actual task. It is too easy for students with dyslexia to go off at a tangent and end up doing a different task.
6. Self-assessment – this looks at whether the student can assess his performance and what he has done well and the areas he can develop.

This process takes a considerable amount of self-knowledge and the student with dyslexia will need support at all these stages. It is important therefore to incorporate these into the tasks and support students at each stage.

DIFFERENTIATION BY ASSESSMENT

It is important to recognize that performance can be assessed by a range of means. It is customary to use written tasks as a means of assessing performance but these can also be differentiated. Differentiation by outcome therefore implies two aspects.

1. The use of a range of modalities – that would mean, for example, using visual, kinaesthetic, investigative discussion and group participation criteria to measure competence. It is crucial that the learning outcomes are well conceived and developed to ensure that a choice of modalities can be used to measure performance.

2. Differentiation of written output as a means of measuring performance – this means that the written output can be displayed in a number of ways – such as journal, chronicle, essay, filling in blanks, interpretation, multiple choice, poem, play and song. Students can be given a choice and they can select the type of assessment they prefer. But it is important that the task is structured for them – so they know which points they need to include and that the assessment should tap into a number of target areas.

For example, if it is a study of a novel you will need to ensure that the assessment task is able to meet the learning outcome as given in the following table.

Topic – Novel study

Learning outcomes for measuring performance				
Learning outcome	Information	Understanding	Vocabulary/ punctuation	Expression, i.e. interest/ style of presentation
Evidence				
Areas for development				

All resources can be useful in some way and they should be used to the maximum effect. Resources for children with dyslexia do not need to cost money – time yes – but it can be time well spent as they can be reused for other children. It is useful to build up a bank of resources so that a choice is available to complement your differentiated materials.

The following are some of the suggested resources that can be used for children with dyslexia. Some may well be expensive but many can be customized by the teacher and these can have a big impact and offer excellent support for children with dyslexia.

DIFFERENTIATION BY RESOURCES

Using resources/strategies

Subject	Resource/strategy	How/why it is used	Effects and benefits
English	Using video or audio materials not as a 'short cut' but as a real alternative – good when first introduced to the theme. Reading materials: ✓ Hi-lo readers ✓ Jumbo font books ✓ Taped books ✓ Electronic books.	It can be multisensory and can provide the student with a clear overview before commencing reading. All of the suggested reading materials can make the text accessible and which is to be used will depend on the needs of the student.	Can help to clarify the background, concepts, ideas and the sequence of events. These materials give the reader a way of accessing text that may not be accessible in a regular book.
Maths	Knowledge and the use of learning styles.	Using sequential/inchworm and holistic/grasshoppers analogy.	The sequential student can be accurate, but the student who would approach problems holistically may be good at identifying patterns and can be more comfortable with mathematical concepts and ideas.
General science	Detailed and labelled plan of the science laboratory and of the topic being taught.	mind maps© can be helpful as it provides a visual plan of the room and the topic being studied – also helps with organization.	Can be consistent with a global learning style and the student does not have to read a lot to study and revise. It is also a personalized way of learning and can be tailored for the individual student.

Subject			
Biology	Abstract words and concepts such as homeostasis, ecosystem and respiration can be displayed as a visual representation.	Can be provided in a notebook with visual illustration or diagram.	Associates the word with the visual representation. This can be reinforcing for the student with dyslexia.
Music	Enlarging a normal size score and using colour or coloured paper. Colour staff can help students identify and decipher particular notes and patterns.	Often students with dyslexia can have musical ability but difficulty in reading music. Reading music involves sequencing and tracking skills so need to highlight the key aspects of the music sheet.	The student will become more keen to use music sheets rather than play the instrument by ear only. Makes reading music more accessible and less challenging.
PE	Provide a list of equipment required.	This can be appended to daily notebook or through emailing the student.	The student will not feel left out as they might if they have forgotten equipment.
History	Engage in a 'print-free' debate and utilize strengths in oral discussion.	This frees the student from having to read thoroughly before engaging in debate. The key points can be provided for them.	Practice in discussion can also have an impact on the pupil's ability to question, infer, deduce, propose and evaluate.

One of the difficulties apart from grammar and spelling which may be experienced by students with dyslexia is the construction and structuring of written work. They may have numerous ideas but lack of structure can mean that some key points may be omitted or that redundant information will be included. In addition, the argument may be jumbled and confusing. You can use many of the principles of differentiation when providing guidance and a structure for these students.

For some students you can provide the structure in an open-ended form whereas other students may need more guidance.

DIFFERENTIATION SUGGESTIONS FOR WRITING

Key heading to be provided:

1. **Preparation** – what they need to think about before embarking on the task. Reading the question thoroughly so they know exactly what is being asked. Check that you have interpreted the question accurately – often there may be more than one way to interpret a question. A KWL chart (see Idea 79) can be used here.
2. **Information** – what they need to know. Create a list of information and/or key points to be covered. Where can the information be found? Create headings and subheadings or perhaps a mind-map.
3. **Construction of the written work** – the sequence, the flow of the main points and the arguments put forward as well as the use of first-person speech, grammar and syntax. From your general key points in your introduction, note down the specific points and examples you will you use to support your points.
4. **Style of writing** – the sentence length, type of sentences and vocabulary used. Use short sentences when constructing arguments and ensure you have used evidence to support your assertions. Try to ensure that each paragraph has a specific focus, is

self-contained and does not repeat what you have already said.

5. **Review** – checking over their work – providing a review checklist can be helpful. Have you identified the key points and the appropriate subpoints that fit into these key points?

While the above framework can be useful it is important that it is contextualized for the subject and topic that is being studied. This means that the teacher can give examples at each of the main stages on what is meant and how it may relate to the topic.

Planning for learning

MANAGING TIME

Young people with dyslexia can have difficulties with time management. At secondary school, pupils are encouraged to work more independently without too much teacher direction, so being aware of time and how to manage it is therefore very important.

PRIORITIZING

Get the pupil to consider all the tasks he needs to do that week. Ask him to code them one to three: one – equal to very important; two – important; and three – can be left until later. Then draw up three columns, one for each category. The pupil must go through each of the lists and place the tasks in rank order, with the most urgent first. Then for each task he must estimate the length of time he thinks he might need to spend on it – this should be in hours, half-days or days.

PLANNING

Now get the pupil to look at his timetable for that week and decide when he will tackle the urgent tasks, and insert them into the timetable. He should also note when he is going to do the task next to the item.

REFLECTION

This is an important part of time management. Reflection involves going through your work at the end of each week and asking questions such as: Did I reach my targets? Did I use my time efficiently? What factors distracted me or prevented me from using my time efficiently? How can I improve on my time management skills? Put questions into columns and use the pupil's answers to help him improve his time management skills.

Vocabulary that is specific to a subject should be thought about at the planning stage and presented to the dyslexic pupil at the time of learning. It is an idea to display a chart with topic-specific vocabulary on the wall. Different colours can be used for different subjects. You can also get the dyslexic pupil to make up his own subject vocabulary and develop this as he meets new topic-specific words. It might be advisable also to indicate a brief meaning beside each word as this can also help with retention.

Some topic-specific vocabulary is shown below:

History	Geography
dynasty	climate
epoch	environment
revolution	terrain
Chemistry	**Biology**
compound	cell
experiment	physiological
mutation	stem
state	
English	**Mathematics**
literature	calculate
metaphor	formulae
syntax	fraction
Art	**Physical education**
easel	words used in specific
sketch	sports such as: ace,
texture	dugout, free kick,
	line judge, offside,
	putt, substitute
Music	**Modern languages**
notes	accent
orchestra	culture
score	customs
sheet	parts of speech

There are a number of computer games and other commercial games that are readily available for dyslexic pupils, but it is a good idea to prepare customized teacher-made games. If the games are made by you they can easily be tailored to reinforce new learning or difficult concepts and can then be used as an overlearning activity.

Game ideas can include:

- Finding the odd word out (see Idea 42)
- Matching the pairs – this could be words with similar sounds or meanings or word endings (see Idea 28)
- Circling letters on the board/worksheet – some letters are more easily confused by the dyslexic pupil than others. It is an idea to get the pupil to circle, for example, all the letters 'p, b, d' in turn. These are often confused as they have visual similarities
- Locating articles beginning with a certain letter or sound
- Words that follow a spelling rule
- Grammar – is it a noun, verb, adjective, adverb?
- Sequencing activities
- Alphabetizing
- Multiple spelling choices – land on an incomplete word and you have to finish the spelling. For example, words with a long 'o' sound – use either 'oa' or 'ow'.

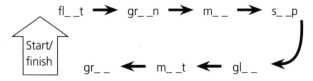

If you keep a supply of blank game boards you can make up a game with relative ease. Photocopy the game board onto heavy paper and use fun shapes and colour to make the games look more inviting. If you keep the game boards in a page protector (or laminate them), they will last a lot longer. You may also want to make your own dice or spinner so that only the numbers 1, 2 and 3 are used as opposed to 1–6 which makes the game go very quickly.

Be creative, just about anything can be practised on a game board.

MATCHING THE PAIRS

This is an example of one of the games suggested in Idea 27. This activity can be beneficial for developing word recognition skills and can also be used with pictures to develop visual discrimination skills.

Find some pairs of words that can be linked for meaning, sound beginning, sound ending or even the same initial letter. Put them into groups along with other words that can be used as distracters – for example, '**tree**, stone, field, **knee**' and '**cup**, broken, **saucer**, hot'. It is a good idea to pilot the lists first and check that there are not any ambiguous items or more than one obvious match. You should try to play this game with the vocabulary the pupil is using at that moment so it helps to reinforce the words. You can also do this to develop concepts and categories as well as linking words together. Pictures can also be used which can be effective with younger children as they have to distinguish two pictures that can go together.

Words that start the same

Or matching for meaning

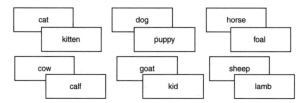

Dyslexic pupils often get tasks and instructions confused, so providing them with a glossary which clearly explains them can be very useful. An example of a key task glossary is shown below:

CALCULATE	Find a numerical answer
COMPARE	Identify differences and similarities
CONTRAST	Compare pieces of information, with a focus on the differences
DEFINE	Give a precise description or meaning for something
DESCRIBE	Provide a series of points in sentences that give an overview of the text or event
DIAGRAM	Construct a graph, chart or drawing or visual portrayal of a piece of information
DISCUSS	Display the points for and against a certain point and provide a conclusion at the end
EXPLAIN	Show that you understand a particular point, text or piece of information
ILLUSTRATE	Use examples to explain a piece of information
JUSTIFY	Provide a statement about why something happened or why you have a certain viewpoint
LIST	Provide a number of items in a sequence
OUTLINE	Present a general summary of an event or a text which will provide the key points
PREDICT	Show the cause and effect of something or the likely outcome of an event
PROVE	Show through a logical progression that something is true
SUMMARIZE	Provide a short account of a text or piece of information that provides the main outline.

It is important to help dyslexic pupils with organization and planning. In secondary school in particular there may be a lot of equipment and materials to remember to bring every day. This could include ruler, timetable, books, pens, pencils, highlighters, paper – plain and ruled – PE kit, materials for specialist subjects like music, food technology, art, food and drink for break times. This can cause difficulties and considerable stress and so the pupil will need some support to ensure that he brings all the necessary equipment each day.

Ask the pupil to make up a chart using lined paper with three columns. One column will have the equipment, another will have a space for a comment that may refer to something particular about the item, and the third column will have space for a tick when the item has been brought. One item should be shown per line, for example, gym kit.

Equipment checklist		
Item	Comment	In place
Gym kit	Remember spare shirt	✓

If there are a lot of remarks in the comment section the pupil can then make a 'to do' list underneath the equipment checklist.

It is important for children with dyslexia to feel that they fit into a group and to obtain experience working in groups or pairs. Quite often they do not and may feel isolated and left out. Yet they can offer so much in all sorts of group activities. It is a good idea to structure the group activity for them otherwise they may not be able to contribute to their full abilities in the group. This can mean ensuring that the composition of the group is balanced and will provide a positive experience for the child with dyslexia. For example, a balanced group should include the following children:

- Good listeners: you need the child who can reflect, listen, facilitate and motivate – often children who are good listeners can do this.
- Good at writing down information and factual detail: this is the child who likes to record information. He may not be too interested in coming up with new ideas but can list the points that are being discussed. He may like to investigate and to find out about things.
- Good in discussion: this is important as the child with dyslexia may fit into this category. They may be able to try out their ideas and their thoughts in the safer discussion environment and obtain feedback from peers at the same time. If there are a few children in the group who like discussion this would make it more effective.
- Like to achieve: you need also to have the child who likes to produce something tangible from the group efforts. This can provide the child with dyslexia with a sense of purpose and a feeling of achievement at the end of the exercise.
- Enjoys creativity: some children can come up with great ideas but have difficulty in putting these into words or in writing. They may also have difficulty sticking to the tasks on hand. This can be the case with children with dyslexia. It is important therefore that in the group they have children who can keep them focused and help to record their ideas. This can provide them with a sense of achievement and a sense of belonging.

It is worth remembering that the responsibility for children with dyslexia should not rest with one teacher but it is a whole-school responsibility. It can be suggested that collaboration is the key to success for children with dyslexia. It is important therefore to ensure that systems are in place to facilitate collaboration. To help with this you can develop teaching goals in conjunction with other teachers or with learning support or teaching assistants. Team teaching can be a component of this and it is important that team teaching is well planned and developed.

You can start with the following:

1. Students needs – short term and long term.
2. Teachers preferences – if there are two teachers involved then each can note the areas they would prefer to teach.
3. The balance of teacher talk and pupils working on their own.
4. How you will implement this in the classroom. For example, one teacher can do the talking part and another can be the monitor and responder to questions. Or one can do the whole-class activities and the other focus on individual children.

It is a good idea to construct a chart to plan and monitor how the lesson has progressed.

It is important at the end of the activity that the two teachers meet to discuss how it went and how it can be improved for the next time.

COLLABORATIVE TEACHING

Collaborative teaching chart

Teacher	Student's learning need	Aim	Materials	Activity	Follow-up
A (Teacher talk)	Develop listening skills	To increase the length of time the student can focus on teacher talk	Position in classroom that minimizes potential distraction	Teacher oral lesson/student chart to note the key points as they are mentioned (the teacher could indicate this is a key point and the student has to note this at the same time)	Differentiated worksheet activities to monitor and assess understanding
B (Prompt and question responder)	"	"	Provide prompts to the student at suitable time	Can give the student cards with key points written on them at appropriate times in the lesson	Individual question and answer session

Learning strategies

It is important when working with dyslexic pupils to identify their preferred learning style – visual, auditory, kinaesthetic or tactile. You can construct questions similar to the ones below to identify their preferences.

Visual

- Do you prefer to find out information from a video rather than listening to someone?
- Do you think of ideas or information in pictures?
- Do you like to draw and illustrate work?

Auditory

- Do you prefer to listen to obtain information?
- Do you like to read a lot of factual information?

Kinaesthetic

- Do you prefer to discuss information with others while you are learning it?
- Do you prefer to learn through role-play and acting?

Tactile

- Do you prefer to learn by building models and making things?

Use these questions to give you some idea of how the pupil prefers to learn. Usually pupils with dyslexia have a preference for visual/kinaesthetic learning.

One of the main reasons why a pupil's learning style is important is that it can be used effectively at the initial stages when tackling new learning. If a task is demanding it is always best to introduce it in a manner that is consistent with the young person's learning preferences. Dyslexic children will respond more readily and it will help to maintain motivation through the difficult initial stages of learning.

If the pupil has a visual/kinaesthetic learning style, introduce new words visually first, getting him to trace the word with his finger in the air and on his desk. He will need to see the word and experience its shape and then practise the way the word sounds.

The same applies when introducing a new novel – the pupil may need to see pictures of the characters, the book jacket or even a video of the book if one is available. If the child has an auditory preference then it is best to begin with an audio tape of the book and then do some reading aloud from the book. Beginning with the best way of learning for a pupil can help to minimize the possibility of failure and loss of motivation.

You can get the student to work this out for themselves by completing a questionnaire, chart or table. Have them indicate what they see as their strengths and encourage them to utilize this when commencing a new topic.

My preferred way of learning is _____.

I find this helpful when I am doing _____.

Things which I have found helpful are _____.

SEQUENCING THE STORY

Sequencing can be difficult for people with dyslexia. A series of illustrations showing the sequence of events can be a good, visual lead in to a story. The sequence can be done with numbers or letters. It is usually better, however, to draw the sequence – using stick figures – or to obtain pictures from the book, if available.

Draw a row of boxes. The pupil will have to fill in each box with a part of the story so you can decide on the number you need. You can start with only two – one for the beginning of the story and one for the end. Then gradually increase the number of boxes to develop the story sequence. Eventually you may want to aim for eight or ten boxes.

As an additional prompt you can put a cue into each box to show the kind of information that is required; for example, the name of the main character or a key word in the plot, or you can provide more detailed cues depending on the level of the pupil's understanding. The pupil can complete the boxes with pictures and a short caption. It is sometimes an idea for the pupil also to put in the page numbers in case he wants to go back and check the information. This can also provide a guide to the sequence.

Overlearning is about repeating the same task, or piece of learning, a number of times to help the pupil consolidate the information. This can be important for remembering spelling rules or facts and ideas which may have to be repeated a number of times before the pupil masters them. Research indicates that dyslexic children need a lot of overlearning as it can take them longer to master new rules, ideas or information.

Make a list of the different ways you could use a new word. This is the basis of overlearning. You need to be aware that overlearning is not the same as rote repetition. For overlearning you should reinforce the new learning through the use of pictures, computer programs, getting the pupil to write a story with the word in it and through discussing the new word and different ways it can be used. It is only through using the word in as many different ways as possible that overlearning can take place. The same strategies apply to any new learning for the dyslexic pupil.

OVERLEARNING

Dyslexic pupils can have difficulty in identifying the key points in a piece of text. As a result they may ramble and digress when reporting on information and may include information that is not entirely relevant. It is therefore important to get them to practise identifying key points.

When tackling new learning, start by presenting the key points. This can be done in the form of a chart, which can also help the pupil to follow the sequence. For example:

Title	Event/information	Key points

At the end of the learning or reading the pupil should also write down what he considers to be the key points – these may be different from those you intended, but it is important to recognize that young people with dyslexia can be quite creative and often see things from a different perspective. It is crucial that this creativity and imaginative thinking is not stifled, so you need to discuss with the pupil his reasons for identifying his key points. The chart can be useful as it provides a source of reference that the pupil can look back to when recapping on the text or revising for exams.

Chunking is a useful strategy with dyslexic pupils as it helps them to remember information more efficiently because it places together pieces of information that are similar. Dyslexic pupils need to practise chunking and ideally they should do this as they are learning new material. This means they have to decide themselves the information they want to chunk.

Select any topic they are working on, for example, in biology – the life cycle of a bird; geography – climate change; English – a novel they are reading; ICT – using a photo/art program; science – recycling waste products; history – the Industrial Revolution. Make a list of the key pieces of information relating to the topic. This could be in phrases or even single words. For example, in the life cycle of the bird the phrases could be: name of the bird family, fertilization, incubation, nesting the young, feeding the young, independence, survival.

Get the pupils to put some of the phrases or words together in one chunk. They now have to look for common factors among these phrases or words and put the common factors underneath. As they practise this activity and are able to identify the common elements, they can then gradually begin to generate the key phrases themselves and make up chunks just from the topic title.

CHUNKING

Dyslexic pupils often have difficulty in utilizing previous knowledge because sometimes they cannot make the connections between new learning and that which they already know. Making these connections and using previous knowledge is, however, necessary to ensure a good understanding of the topic and of the ideas and concepts involved.

Begin by asking the pupil what he already knows about the topic. Ask how he knows that information. Identify the new information that will need to be learnt and place this in a blank box titled 'New learning' on the pupil's worksheet. Then help the pupil to compare the new learning ideas with his previous knowledge of the topic. Show him how much learning he has acquired. Get him to use this process when tackling a new piece of learning by constructing two columns called 'What I already know' and 'What I need to find out'. This will give the pupil a framework for learning the new material.

There are many other activities that may help students make connections about what they already know or understand about a topic to what they will be learning.

Ways of using what I already know to help me understand!

KWL chart – see Idea 79.

Five senses chart – this works particularly well for settings. What would you feel, smell, hear, taste, see if you were to spend a day . . . . (in the forest, at the beach, at a ranch, etc.)

Wondering web – create a web of questions that you want to answer? During or after the reading you can fill in the questions.

Chapter chart – look at the title of the chapters and make predictions about what will happen next.

Visuals, charts and diagrams – providing graphics is a quick and easy way to activate prior knowledge. It is a method that is often used with younger students but can also be very valuable for high school students.

Encourage pupils to use headings and subheadings in written work to help provide them with a structure. Often learners with dyslexia have difficulty in developing a structure and need guidance with this.

To begin with these headings and subheadings can be summaries of the events. Have the pupil summarize different parts of the story or information that is being learnt and then note one key word or phrase that can describe the summary. Once that has been done, explain to the pupil that the word or phrase can be the heading or subheading. It is often easier to do it this way than to get them to identify the heading words as dyslexic pupils can have a word-finding difficulty. This method will give them a context to help identify the key words for headings.

DEVELOPING A STRUCTURE

1. Developing a structure for identifying key words

Summary of events Paragraph 1	Summary of events Paragraph 2	Summary of events Paragraph 3
———— ———— ———— ————	———— ———— ———— ————	———— ———— ———— ————

2. Subheadings

Phrase to describe Paragraph 1	Phrase to describe Paragraph 2	Phrase to describe Paragraph 3
———— ————	———— ————	———— ————

3. Heading

Word or phrase used to describe all 3 paragraphs
———————— ————

Ask the dyslexic pupil what type of environment he prefers to work in. You can use headings for this for your own guidance, such as sound, light, temperature, classroom layout. Questions you can ask include:

- Do you prefer to work when it is quiet or with background noise?
- Do you like to talk with people while you are working or work quietly by yourself?
- Do you like to listen to music while you are working?
- Do you prefer to work with a dim table light or bright lights?
- Do you like to work with a jacket or fleece on or do you prefer a T-shirt or something cool?
- Do you like a lot of space in the classroom?
- Do you like to have your own desk and work space or are you happy sharing this with someone else?

It is an idea to feed the results of this back to the pupil so that he can have some appreciation of his learning preferences – it is never too early to give pupils an insight into this.

This can also be done with very young children by using pictures instead of words. For example, show a picture of a child reading on his own and another picture of children reading together at the same table, or a picture of a child reading with a table lamp and one with a child reading with a bright light – then ask the child which he prefers. Do this for all the questions listed above.

You can also add to the list items relating to the time of day and whether they like to move around while learning. Many children with dyslexia prefer some mobility when they are learning, rather than being seated all the time. Ask if they prefer a chair with a back or sitting on the floor or on a bean bag. Dyslexic children often prefer to sit on the floor or on a bean bag as it is less formal than sitting in an upright chair.

It is important to try to increase the reading fluency of dyslexic pupils. This can be done through activities that develop both word recognition skills and reading comprehension skills. A good level of comprehension can also compensate for difficulties in reading accuracy.

It is useful to develop games that can assist in the development of word recognition and word meaning. One good game to play is 'find the odd word out'. Give the pupils a list of words where one is different from the rest. They have to scan all the words and recognize the one that is different. As well as applying reading accuracy skills, they are also reading for meaning. This activity can be done with words they are currently using in a class topic, as this can help to reinforce learning of new words. A timed element can also be introduced and this can help to develop fluency.

Example 1

Breeds of dogs
Poodle
Cocker spaniel
Golden Retriever
Turtle
German shepherd
Border Collie
Beagle
Dalmatian
Husky

Example 2

Team Sports
Hockey
Football
Baseball
Dodge ball
Helmet
Basketball
Volleyball
Lacrosse

Many learners with dyslexia find it easier to use visual skills for processing information than other modalities, such as auditory skills. Their visual pathways can be more highly developed and they can understand and retain information more easily if it is learnt visually. They can also use their visual skills to develop creative ideas and this can help with expressive writing. There are many strategies which can be used in different areas of the curriculum to help the student with dyslexia utilize their visual strengths. Some are shown below:

For maths the student can make visual facts cards for the properties of different shapes. This can be their own creation and they can design it their way. You will have to give them the shape you want them to remember. This can be done visually as the example below shows.

You can also use this visualization strategy with other concepts such as proportion and scale.

Curved

Angular

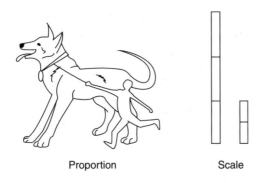

Proportion   Scale

For creative writing, visual skills can be a great boost in helping the student develop a story-line and providing details about size, shape, colour and movement which can all be included in the story. They can start with a word, sentence, picture or an idea. They then have to visualize it and describe the word or idea.

Visuals can also be used to help the student organize information such as mind-mapping (see Idea 48), the use of highlighters or bold letters to make key points stand out, to connect ideas, to help remember use symbols and to identify key words. Encourage the student to use colours as much as possible when developing visualization techniques. This will take practice for some students and it can be gradually introduced using simple topics and ideas.

Practice in using visual skills can develop skills in visual imagery as well as sophisticated and effective mnemonics which can also help with memory. It can be fun and useful in all curriculum subjects. In science with cell shapes and cell division, in biology with plants and animals. It can be used in all subjects as a study skill strategy that can also help to explain and provide some clarity in the topic being studied.

Dyslexic pupils can have difficulty in planning, preparing and writing essay questions. As well as practice they need some guidance in the sequence they should follow. Quite often they have difficulty in making a start to an essay, and they may need some prompts on what to do next. It can be useful to provide a plan to keep them on track.

Provide a series of headings with directions and questions that can prompt them on what they should be doing when. They can also use this type of plan as a checklist after they have finished the essay to ensure that they have considered all the different areas.

PREPARATION

- Examine the question, topic or issue.
- Ask yourself what the question means.
- Write down what you think the question is asking.
- What do you already know about the topic?
- What do you still have to find out?
- What is your answer to the question?
- What detail would support your answer?

GATHERING

- What sort of information do you need?
- Where will you find it?
- What are the key points?
- Keep a record of where you obtained information.
- Organize your notes into sections and chunks.

STRUCTURING

- Develop an essay plan.
- Note the key points for the introduction.
- Interpret the question.
- Note the key points in each part of the essay.
- Which examples will you use to support your points?
- Make sure your conclusion is a firm answer to the question and that it relates to your introduction.

CHECKING

- Identify the subheadings.
- Make sure all notes fit into a subheading.
- Write out the key points from your essay.
- Put some detail under each key point.
- Check your key points with those in the essay.
- What are the implications from your key points?
- Remember, writing notes is an active way of learning not passive.

WRITING

- Write simply and directly.
- Limit your sentence length.
- Ensure that each paragraph has a focus.
- Take care to acknowledge the work of others, and include references.
- Proofread for meaning, then for grammar.
- Ask yourself if the presentation is clear enough.

LEARNING STYLES ACROSS THE CURRICULUM

Learning styles are about recognizing the preferences individuals have for learning and teachers need to develop appropriate learning tools, strategies, methods and materials to help students succeed. Learning styles are best adopted as a whole-school approach.

You can do this by using a chart such as the one below – the idea of this is to get everyone in the school tuned into the benefits of learning styles. The key points in the chart below are the learning environment, the connections between new learning and previous learning, activities, and the whole picture – a global overview of the topic. These points are important for learning and most teachers would appreciate that. What you need to do now is to convert those to learning styles by showing how each can be accommodated within a learning styles programme. It is important to consider the environment in learning styles and the following points need to be acknowledged.

- The classroom design and layout should accommodate to features such as colour, sound and music and design.
- Some learning environments may be more suited to left hemisphere learners while others to right hemisphere.
- Environmental preferences can be considered following discussion with the learner or through observation of the learner in different settings.

It is also important to acknowledge that learning styles can overlap and complement other aspects of learning such as multiple intelligence, metacognition, thinking styles and teaching styles and these can lend themselves to whole-school cross-curricular initiatives. Knowledge of learning style can help the student become more aware of individual preferences and can lead to metacognitive awareness and acknowledging learning styles can help to promote skills that can extend beyond school.

An example of this is shown in the following table:

Learning styles across the curriculum

Environment	Metacognitive	Task	Learning style
Create a supportive learning environment	Connect/ activate previous learning	Activity (action – doing something)/ writing	Offer the big picture
Rearrange desks	Thinking skills	Listening	Step-by-step approach
Focus on wall displays	Encourage self-questioning – can be done in pairs	Discussing	Group work

It is crucial that factors associated with learning style are taken into consideration in planning and in assessment.

The example above looks at modality preferences but learning styles can incorporate cognitive, affective and physiological aspects such as those noted below:

- Cognitive dimension includes modality preferences, attention, memory processes and concept development
- Affective dimension includes personality variables that can influence learning such as persistence and perseverance, frustration and tolerance, curiosity, locus of control, achievement motivation, risk taking, cautiousness, competition, cooperation, reaction to reinforcement and personal interests
- Physiological dimension includes time of day rhythms, need for mobility and environmental elements.

Memory
strategies

Doing it is better than hearing it! Dyslexic children are usually experiential learners – they need to engage in learning actively. Passive learning will not be successful for them. This means that tasks need to involve making or constructing things. Role-play, games and group activities are successful because the pupils are actively learning. Computer games are also good because they involve a degree of activity. When planning a lesson, make a detailed chart of the task that is to be carried out and tick off the aspects of the learning that involve activity. It is important to ensure that there is a balance between active learning and passive learning. Active learning can involve the following:

- Writing an account
- Performing a play
- Discussing in groups
- Investigating a problem
- Conducting an experiment
- Constructing a wall display
- Composing and performing a song or poem
- Reconstructing a battle
- Making an audio tape
- Illustrating a story
- Role-play and games.

One activity that works well and involves active learning is to get pupils to compose a song about learning and how they learn. They can use the tune to well-known songs or nursery rhymes and fit in words that are associated with their own learning.

To start with you can give them some basic introduction to the anatomy of the brain; for example, indicating that it consists of two hemispheres and parts of the brain specialize in language, while other areas focus on visual information. You can go into this in some detail, depending on the age of the pupils. It is a good idea also to mention the emotional part of the brain and the need to feel good when learning.

Then help the pupils to select a tune – some examples can be given but young people are usually very good at finding a rhythm and tune they can use. Rap songs are often very popular.

Do not give them too long to compose the song – they can usually do it quite quickly – but it is useful to give them some of the key ideas about learning and some of the main words and terms relating to the brain. Some of the key words can include learning style, learning actively, learning lists, writing things down, mind-maps, brain cells, hemispheres, best time of day for learning, music, lighting.

This activity provides a good opportunity for pupils to learn actively and for the whole class to participate, not just the dyslexic pupils.

47

RELAX

Children will learn more effectively when they are relaxed. This is especially the case for those with dyslexia who can become anxious about school work but may not show it. Relaxation activities include the following:

- Eyes closed, listening to classical music
- Visualization techniques
- Allocating time for a favourite activity without any form of structure or demand
- Exercises involving body flexing, such as yoga
- Games and sports
- Puzzles.

The key point regarding relaxation is that the pupil must have a free choice and be able to choose his own form of relaxation. For example, for some children reading may be a good form of relaxation, but this may not be the case for dyslexic pupils.

To prepare for relaxation, ensure that all items that may be distracting are out of sight. If relaxation is to take place in the classroom, clear the desks first and put away any clutter. If the relaxation activity is involving music and visualization, it is best to dim the lights as this will minimize distraction. When you give instructions, speak in a softer voice than usual, and when coming out of the relaxation period, increase the volume of your voice gradually and slowly break off the relaxation time.

You can include the whole class in relaxation sessions, everyone will benefit and the dyslexic pupil will not feel singled out.

Mind-mapping can be a useful strategy because it uses visual skills and can provide opportunities for lateral thinking and creativity. It also helps the learner organize the information into headings and categories. It can take a range of forms, but it is best to start with a theme or event that the pupil is familiar with, such as how he spent the weekend. This is preferable to mind-mapping a book or a piece of information he is working on. Eventually you can work towards that, but a topic such as 'my weekend' is very personal and the pupil will have recent memories of it. It is a good idea to provide the pupil with a plan for the mind-map.

Ask the pupil to make a mind-map of his weekend. Try to follow the sequence below to begin with. Once he has done this he can add other items to the mind-map. Remember this is his own personal mind-map and will very likely be different from others in the class – even if the child has done similar things at the weekend, he may put it down in a different way. There is no right or wrong way of doing this. The important point is what works best for the pupil.

Next, ask the pupil to make a list of the main types of activities and events that took place under headings such as house, outside leisure, money, friends, school work and other activities. Then break each of these down into more detailed lists, such as house – vacuuming, preparing food, helping younger brother get dressed, talking with family. Each of these can be broken into more detail, for example, with preparing food, the details might be making breakfast, mixing up breakfast juice, and so on. Visuals can be added to the list, but ensure that they are the pupil's own representation of the information.

Once he has done this type of mind-map a few times you can then try some school topics such as history and specific details such as battles or kings, or a chemistry experiment or a country he has studied in geography.

WRITE, RECITE AND REPEAT

One of the main difficulties experienced by dyslexic pupils involves the use of short- and long-term memory. It is important, therefore, that pupils have a personal notebook, write down notes and make a daily 'to do' list.

When noting the information in his book the pupil could:

- write it down – the actual process of writing can help strengthen the kinaesthetic memory
- recite it to himself, or to others – this strengthens the memory through both the speech and auditory channels
- repeat it a number of times – this can help to absorb the information through the auditory channel
- annotate the notes with visual symbols and key words – this helps to develop the visual skills.

This method is multisensory as it involves the full range of learning skills – seeing, listening, writing, saying and doing. Pupils can use this write, recite and repeat method for most areas of work involving memory, such as spelling rules, history facts and mathematics problems.

This involves

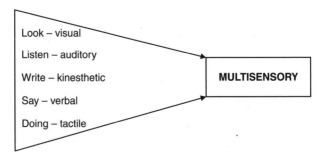

Look – visual
Listen – auditory
Write – kinesthetic
Say – verbal
Doing – tactile

MULTISENSORY

It is best to review notes the same day as the memory trace recedes very quickly. If the pupil waits until the next day or the end of the week the information will be less meaningful.

Make a time each day for reviewing that day's work and any notes that have been made. It is more likely that the dyslexic pupil will be able to read notes he has written himself – even if the spelling is wrong – rather than read someone else's notes.

Ensure that not too much information is attempted to be learnt in one sitting. The key to minimizing loss of information from memory is little and often. That means that study should be in short bouts and frequently. After each short period of study review the notes before moving on to the next piece of information.

To review the notes the student should ask himself some questions about the notes. Prepare a list of questions for the student to refer to.

Questions

What are the notes about?
What new information do they provide?
What strategies should I use to remember the
      information?
How can I reorganize them to make them more
      valuable to me?
Do they have headings and subheadings?
How will I separate the information if I colour code
      the page?

Finally, the pupil should be able to write a summary of the notes. It is best to do this every few pages or less.

Dyslexic pupils often develop what is known as 'learnt helplessness'. The pupil convinces himself that he cannot do a particular task. Once 'learnt helplessness' has been experienced it is difficult to undo, so it is important to try to prevent this through the development of a positive attitude and a high level of self-esteem.

Provide learners with tasks that are achievable and ensure they experience some success in what they are doing. Success is the key to a positive attitude, and providing appropriate tasks is the key to success.

Select a task that the dyslexic pupil finds challenging. Identify the particular aspects of that task that he is experiencing difficulty with and write out the main barriers within the task that are preventing him from succeeding. Once you have identified each barrier, break these down into smaller more manageable tasks. Prepare a checklist showing each of these tasks and make each task a learning objective. Then teach each objective and as he succeeds he can tick each one off on the checklist. This type of checklist can be useful when teaching reading and spelling.

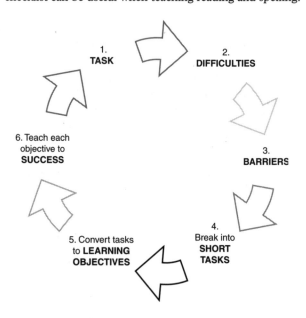

1. **TASK**

2. **DIFFICULTIES**

3. **BARRIERS**

4. Break into **SHORT TASKS**

5. Convert tasks to **LEARNING OBJECTIVES**

6. Teach each objective to **SUCCESS**

Young people with dyslexia need to consolidate new learning and this can take a considerable amount of time. One way to do this is to use the new information that is being learnt in as many different ways as possible.

When the pupil is learning to spell a new word it is important that he uses the word and tries to construct sentences with it. Try to ensure that the pupil carries this out daily, even during weekends, as missing even one day can mean that the new word will be lost. Continue doing this until the pupil has automaticity in the new word or whatever activity is being learnt. Automaticity can be evident when the pupil can do the activity or use the word correctly and spontaneously on a number of occasions – usually around six to eight times. As an additional reinforcer, a mnemonics spelling list can be encouraged (see Idea 54). For example, 'because' can be remembered by the mnemonic 'big elephants can add up sums easily' and 'necessary' by 'one collar, two sleeves' (this can help to reinforce the one 'c' and the double 's' in necessary).

This process can be used with reading and spelling new words and also to learn new information – for example, historical facts in history or features of different countries in geography.

New word

pier

Sentences

The seagulls were crowding round the pier.

The stormy waves were battering against the pier.

On a sunny day there are a lot of people on the pier watching the birds and the sea life.

REINFORCING LEARNING

Self-knowledge can be the key to an effective memory. Dyslexic pupils can become 'bogged down' in the mechanics of a task and unaware of how they actually carried it out. It is important, therefore, to help them recognize the learning processes they have been using. This can also relate to the learning environment and they should be encouraged to develop an awareness of the environments that are best suited for them and those which are not.

To help the dyslexic pupil develop and become aware of himself as a learner try this exercise with him.

- Make a list of the things around you that can distract you when learning.
- List those aspects that are the most distracting.
- Indicate why you think these aspects are distracting.
- Is it possible to avoid these factors?
- Show how they can be avoided.
- Now list those aspects that help you concentrate better when learning.
- Why do you think they help you concentrate better?
- Is it the same for every type of learning or does it depend on what type of activity you are doing?
- Now make a self-study plan from your responses above that will show your learning preferences.

Activity	Aspects that help concentration	Distractions
Reading		
Spelling		
Writing		
Memory work		
Brainstorming		

There are a number of different ways of constructing a mnemonic activity, but it is best if the actual mnemonic comes from the learner himself. The general rule is that the pupil should construct it from his own imagination, and the more ridiculous the associations are, the easier it is to remember them.

One of the most well-known mnemonics is the body peg system. This involves identifying parts of the body – hair, head, ears, eyes, neck, shoulders, hands, fingers, stomach, chest, legs, knees, feet, toes – and associating each one with an object or phrase to help remember them. Mnemonics can also be invented using items in a room, such as table, chair, wall, window, floor, door, desk, drawer, cupboard, or objects well known to the child, such as football, field, phone, backpack, friends.

One example of a spelling mnemonic is 'doubt' – 'do you believe that'. Try to create mnemonics that make sense for the word and possibly explain the meaning of the word. If the mnemonic is relevant and meaningful to the word itself, it will be more easily remembered by the student. Mnemonics can also help for remembering, for example, the top left-hand side of a keyboard – 'qwerty', or that 'stationery' is spelt with an 'e' for envelope.

It is best to emphasize the fun aspect of the activity, which is why the most ridiculous associations can be more easily remembered. It is also an idea for children to work in pairs or groups to begin with to ensure that no one is left behind. This can be an effective strategy for dyslexic pupils as they often have a good imagination and it helps to boost their memory of lists, especially items that have to be remembered in sequence.

ORGANIZING YOUR MIND

Information can be remembered more effectively if it is organized at the point of learning. Dyslexic pupils are often very concerned about getting the information down but only try to understand and learn it later. When they go back to review the information they have often forgotten the context and may not be able to understand the information fully. It is more effective to try to get them to understand the information as they are writing it down. This requires organizational skills and practice at taking notes.

Get the pupil to practise this using the formula below.
Input – taking information in. The pupil needs to organize the information as he is taking it in by reading, listening or watching. He can put it into headings, subheadings or his own method of coding information – for example, bullet points or colour coding.
Cognition – processing or learning the information. The pupil puts the information into categories or groups of ideas. This will relate to what is already known about the new learning. At this stage he needs to absorb the new information into his existing understanding of the topic that is being studied.
Output – reporting on the information. Now the pupil can prepare the information in some order for writing about it or for presenting it orally:

- Introduction
- Key points
- Essential information
- Implications
- Additional information needed/questions still to be answered
- Concluding comments.

Any type of information will be recalled more effectively if it is organized – this is the key to a good memory.

Acronyms can be a useful tool for dyslexic learners. They can often remember an acronym more easily than a piece of text. There are many types of acronyms and they can be used for different purposes. In the examples below, the letters of an entire word each stand for a concept to memorize and recall.

Taking notes from an oral presentation: SLANT

S: Sit up.
L: Lean forward.
A: Activate your 'thinking machine'.
N: Name (verbalize softly) the key information.
T: Track the talker for non-verbal and verbal information.

Taking a test/answering examination questions: REMEMBER

R: Read questions carefully.
E: Eliminate tough questions and go for easy ones first.
M: Mark the key words to focus in on the question.
E: Eliminate irrelevant information that crosses your mind.
M: Mark down the key words of what you want to say.
B: Breathe to give your brain/thinking machine oxygen.
E: Estimate the time you can take to answer the question.
R: Respond and recheck your response.

Taking a test: listen and respond in writing: SPENT

S: Sit up front.
P: Pre-read the questions to anticipate the topic.
E: Eliminate panic thoughts and focus on the topic.

N: Normalize breathing.

T: Trace key words orally and look for them in print.

(Adapted from Crombie and Schneider, 2004, *Dyslexia and Foreign Language Learning*, David Fulton Publishers, with permission.)

Reading and reading comprehension

DEVELOPING PHONOLOGICAL AWARENESS SKILLS

WHAT IS PHONOLOGICAL AWARENESS?

Phonological awareness is the awareness of sounds in spoken language. Phonological awareness should involve being able to hear and manipulate sounds in oral language.

- ✓ The ability to hear and manipulate spoken sounds.
- ✓ It is an auditory exercise without the grapheme representation.
- ✓ Symbols of letters are not present for demonstration of phonological awareness.

Each skill should be introduced individually, from simple to complex and then practised before introducing the next skill. These are auditory exercises with no words shown; it is not reading. The teacher says the phrase and the child repeats it. It can be fun and more interesting for the child to include graphics. This can be done individually with small visuals or in a group with larger visuals.

Phonological awareness skills include:

- Awareness of whole words: It is good to provide the child with a way of counting the words. You can have each child count out the words with a drum stick or you may want to have each child use counters in circles. They would place one counter per word in the circle. Give each child a strip of paper with five or six circles on it and with five or six counters.

at the park – three words

computer game – two words

three curious little dogs – four words

- Awareness of syllables: The same idea of using counters can be used here to count syllables. Use the same strips but different counters to represent a syllable. Choose words with varying numbers of syllables from one to four or more depending on the child.

study – two syllables

indication – four syllables
computer – three syllables
shoe – one syllable
sister – two syllables

Being able to divide the syllables correctly is not the primary focus here. Rather it is being able to hear that there are one, two, three (or more) syllables in a word which is a different skill from being able to hear how many different words there are in a sentence or phrase.

- Discrimination (fin, fish, fast: What was the same sound?): This skill is not about being able to read and 'see' these words. The teacher would read the words; the students are listening to the sounds. It is helpful to provide pictures of the words (but not the word itself).
- Rhyming: bar, car, far, . . . : What is another word that will rhyme or the words bar, snack, car, far . . . Which word didn't belong?

- Segmentation: fun = /f/ /u/ /n/ – how many sounds are in this word? The teacher provides the word and the child listens and segments.
- Blending phonemes (/s/ /u/ /n/ = sun): Here the sounds are provided by the teacher and the child produces the word.
- Deletion (stand – /t/ = sand): Teacher says the word 'stand' and then asks the child to produce the word without one of the sounds. 'Now say the word without the /t/ sound'.
- Manipulation (fin: change /i/ to /a/ = fan): The teacher says the word 'fin' and then asks the child to say the word again, replacing one sound with another. 'Now say the word but change the /i/ sound to an /a/ sound'. Child says 'fan'.

The term 'sight words' can be used to refer to words that are recognized instantly, without hesitation and usually includes both phonetic and non-phonetic, high-frequency words. However, phonetic words can be taught using phonic rules and codes so only non-phonetic words will be referred to here. For example, the word 'what' is a non-phonetic word; it cannot be sounded out. It is necessary to explicitly teach these words and for children to memorize the spelling therefore they will likely need a considerable amount of overlearning. Following are some activities for overlearning sight words:

- Tracing the letters: Glitter glue is a great way to make these quickly. Have the student trace over each letter in the word, saying the letter as they trace it and then saying the whole word. Using red for the letters will signal to the child that they have to stop and think because these words cannot be sounded out.

what

'w' 'h' 'a' 't' spells 'what' – tracing and saying together is more powerful than just doing one or the other. Have the child do this at least five times for each word.

- Sky writing: Draw the letters in the sky with your arm straight and your index finger pointing out. Always have the child say each letter as they are writing it in the sky and then say the whole word. Always have the child use the hand they write with.
- Create a reading deck of sight words: There is no teaching here; this is a review of words they are able to read. Have the student read the words daily. This should only take about 3 minutes as the reading drill should be fast and fluent. As new non-phonetic words are learned, add them to the reading deck so the size of the deck continues to increase as more are known. Print the words in red so it signals to the child that these are words that cannot be sounded out. If the child makes as error, tell them what it says and have them repeat the word and then trace the letters, saying the letters as they trace. Then place the card a in the deck again, about ten cards back, so it comes up again.

Being able to read text fluently helps to develop comprehension, but dyslexic children often have a difficulty with this.

Increase reading fluency by asking pupils to read a page at their own pace. They should then read the page again and underline all the key words, then read only those words that are underlined. Try this several times – they may also note down the key words – then try it with a different page without underlining the key words. Discuss with them what they have read as soon as possible, and finish by summarizing the key points of the text.

This can be turned into a game by giving the pupils less time than they need to read the page or text – you can even make it something quite ridiculous like 45 seconds. That way the pupils have to concentrate only on the main words. This is good for dyslexic pupils because they often have difficulty with the small, less important words like 'for' and 'from' and may spend a lot of time pronouncing these words, even though they may not add much to the meaning of the text. Trying to read every word accurately, even small words, can disrupt the flow of the reading and affect comprehension. By turning this into a fun game you can help to minimize any anxiety and make it challenging for everyone in the class so the dyslexic child will not feel in any way different.

Another activity is to provide the pupils with a strip of paper with a phrase on it. Ensure it is a phrase that they are able to decode as the goal is fluency and not word attack skills. For example, if the topic is about a football game the phrase might be, 'The referee blew his whistle.' Once they have looked at it they need to turn it text side down on the desk and then say what they have read. This not only aids fluency, it also helps dyslexic pupils to understand that reading should sound like talking. This can also be good for helping to overcome any barriers and anxieties the child may experience concerning reading.

Encourage dyslexic children to read a book that is above their reading level as this will provide them with an expanded and richer vocabulary and also help to extend their comprehension skills. This can be done as a shared reading activity with other children, with adults, or using a taped book.

Present the new words that pupils will experience in the reading. Look the words up in the dictionary and get the pupils to write sentences using the new words. They should be given an opportunity to discuss the new word in each sentence. This can be the first stage of shared reading. In shared reading the child and the adult (teacher, parent or sometimes another pupil) take turns in reading. If the child hesitates on a word the adult should say the word, as the main point of the exercise is to extend language experience and not to decode. Taped books are very useful for this. Many books are available commercially in audio form, but you could compile your own bank of taped books. It is important that this becomes a school resource that can be shared and extended by all staff. This may also be an activity in which the school librarian can participate.

EXTENDING LANGUAGE EXPERIENCE

Paired reading involves the adult and the child reading aloud at the same time. It is, however, a specific, structured technique.

The child should choose a book. Then both adult and child read all the words out loud together, with the adult modulating their speed to match that of the child, while giving a good model of competent reading. The child must read every word and when the child says a word wrong, the adult just tells him the correct way to say the word. The child then repeats the word correctly and the pair carry on. Saying 'no' and giving phonic and other prompts is forbidden. The adult does not jump in and correct the child straight away. The rule is that the adult pauses and gives the child 4 or 5 seconds to see if he will put it right by himself.

The key principles of paired reading are as follows:

- The child selects the reading material
- The adult and child read together
- The programme is carried out consistently
- Distractions should be minimal
- Praise is used as reinforcement
- The story and pictures are discussed at the end.

The two principal stages of paired reading are: reading together and reading alone.

Reading together – this is when the parent/teacher and child read all the words aloud, with the adult adjusting the speed so that the pair are reading in harmony. The adult does not allow the child to become stuck at a word and if this happens will simply say the word to the child. This process, together with discussion, can help the child obtain meaning from the text and therefore enjoy the experience of language and of reading.

Reading alone – this occurs when the child becomes more confident at reading aloud. The adult can either read more softly, thus allowing the child to take the lead, or remain quiet. This can be built up gradually to allow the child's confidence to grow. When the child stumbles at this stage, the adult immediately offers the word and then continues reading with the child again, until he gains enough confidence to read unaided.

One of the important aspects of paired reading and indeed any reading activity is praise – remember to look pleased when the child succeeds using this technique.

Keeping a paired reading diary, such as the following table, is a good way for the child to acknowledge his success with reading.

My paired reading diary

Date	Title of book	What I liked about the book!	Would I recommend it to a friend Yes/No

Phrasing is an important part of becoming a fluent reader. As fluent readers, this is something we do naturally. Grouping words together, as in normal speech, means that reading should sound like talking. Children with dyslexia may struggle to cluster portions of the text together in a way that makes sense. They will likely need practice reading in phrases as opposed to reading word by word. It is important to model or demonstrate how grouping words together should sound.

Activities to promote phrasing:

- Provide a heading and ask the child to brainstorm lists of phrases.
- Complete sentences with a phrase
  I finished my homework _____ (when)
  The child may respond by writing 'before I played outside' or 'after dinner'.
- Group words together by lightly scooping appropriate phrases with a pencil.

Yesterday morning we went for a walk on the beach.

- Provide phrases on strips of paper and ask the child to organize the phrases into a sentence.

to the library		said to her class		to go
	it is time		Ms. Green	

- Ask the child to break up a sentence into phrases. You could provide sentence strips and ask the child to cut the sentences into phrases, write the phrases on another sheet of paper or simply use a slash between phrases.

Ms Green
said to her class
it is time
to go
to the library.
Ms Green/said to her class/it is time/to go/to the library.

- Break up a paragraph into phrases (same as above but with a whole paragraph).

On a sunny Sunday afternoon
the young girl
asked her mom
if she could
take the dog
for a walk.
Her mom
was worried
about her
going alone.
She asked
the girl's brother
to go with her.
The boy
was annoyed
because he wanted
to play
on the computer.

The best way to consolidate vocabulary is to use the vocabulary in as many different contexts as possible. Most adjectives can be used in different subject areas, for example, history, geography, science and English. It is a good idea to target some adjectives from words the pupil is currently learning and to highlight these in the different curricular areas. This activity can also be used to highlight different aspects of grammar, such as adjectives, nouns and adverbs. This is important as it helps to transfer learning to different subject areas and helps the learner use the same word in different ways. Try to develop the list of vocabulary to be consolidated alongside different activities. Some examples are shown below:

Target adjectives   *Consolidation activity*

bright   describing colours of liquids (science)
             studying the weather (geography)
light   describing weight (science) describing
             weather, for example, light shower
             (geography)
substantial (most subject areas)

Target nouns

fight   describing battles (history)
             vocabulary used in some novels
             (English)
key   the key to a diagram (science) or in
             social subjects where the information on
             the page can be developed using a key.

It is important to look for opportunities in all subjects areas to consolidate vocabulary. It is this consolidation that provides the dyslexic pupil with overlearning experiences that help to reinforce new learning (see Idea 36 for details on overlearning).

A vocabulary consolidation list can also be used as a checklist so you can monitor the extent of the vocabulary that is being reinforced. It also emphasizes the importance of cross-curricular communication in the secondary sector.

Teaching reading comprehension requires careful thought and planning ahead particularly if a teacher is reaching different levels of comprehension. It is necessary for the teacher to read the text ahead of time in order to prepare a lesson the student will fully benefit from.

Following are some ways to plan for comprehension:

- Pre-teach vocabulary: This requires the teacher to pre-read the text and to then select all the vocabulary the child may struggle with. This should include words that the child will struggle to pronounce, such as proper nouns, as well as words they will not understand. Write the words on cards, in a large clear font, to be presented to the child before the reading begins. It is helpful, particularly for younger children, to provide a graphic along with the word. Show the word to the child and say the word and tell the meaning. This is a teaching step, not a guessing game on the part of the child.

COMPREHENSION PLANNING

muskrat

- Phrasing and scooping: Prepare phrases from the text that you feel the child may struggle with. This could be either because of the pronunciation of a word or words or it may contain a word or words the child will not understand. For example, 'generally inhabits wetlands' describes where a muskrat lives. All three of these words may need explaining. The word 'inhabit' may seem obvious if you have been discussing the 'habitation' of animals but the variation of the word will likely need to be explained. Have the child read the phrase and then discuss what it means, each word and all together. This way when the child comes to the phrase in the text it will be familiar and the child will not have to stop.
- Prepare questions ahead of time at all levels of comprehension: Coming up with questions at a literal level of comprehension is quite easy and can be done on the spot. However, coming up with inferential questions or questions that require some critical or creative thought will often take careful consideration on the part of the teacher.
- Consider the following areas to discuss ahead of reading to enhance comprehension:

For the reading of fictional material

- Title
- Setting – time and place
- Background knowledge that will help the reader understand the context
- Characters, including names
- Main events
- Sequence of events
- Resolution and conclusion

For the reading of factual material

- Title, overview, summary and conclusion
- Pictures and diagrams
- Background knowledge
- Terminology/vocabulary

COMPREHENSION MONITORING

Comprehension is the ability to get meaning from what we have read. Comprehension monitoring goes further than this and is the ability of a reader to know when he is understanding what he is reading and when he is not. If pupils with good comprehension monitoring do not understand the text they will usually know why, and what they need to do to remedy this.

A good reader will read automatically and smoothly so long as there is good comprehension. They do not usually have to devote constant attention to evaluating their own understanding. When the understanding of material is not complete the reader will do one of many things: stop and reread more carefully, slow down allowing more processing time, look up words in the dictionary, analyse phrases or sentences for exact meaning, draw on previous knowledge, seek clarification for a particular trouble spot, and so on. In other words, a good reader will engage in comprehension monitoring.

There are many different ways in which comprehension can break down. There may be new words in the text that the reader has not come across before, or words that do not make sense in the context. Sentences may seem vague or ambiguous, or the reader may have a lack of prior knowledge of the subject and lose the meaning.

Teachers must model and practise techniques with the pupil, as comprehension monitoring doesn't come naturally or easily. They must teach pupils to:

- track their thinking
- notice when they lose focus
- stop and go back
- reread
- identify what is confusing
- select the best strategy.

The pupils can ask themselves:

- Where did I lose track?
- Does this make sense?
- Can I say it in my own words?
- What do I think will happen next?

It's a good idea to write these questions on cards for the pupils as they should not be expected to remember them, no matter how many times they have gone through this exercise. If they are not able to answer these questions, they must use a 'fix-up strategy' to get back on track. For example:

- Go back and reread
- Look up the word or words in the dictionary
- Clarify a concept
- Ask questions.

Create cue cards for the students to refer to so they don't have to try to remember what to do. It may be helpful to include visuals on the cards so they can refer to the picture icon rather than reading each card.

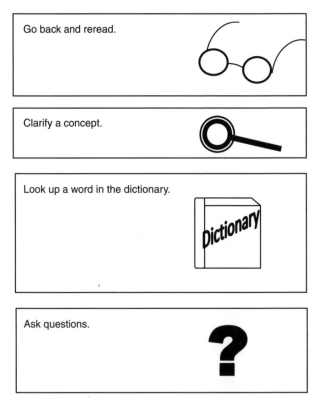

Encourage pupils to check their own understanding and bring active meaning to the text. This technique works best when the pupil is able adequately to decode the chosen text.

The teacher goes first, modelling the read-aloud and think-aloud process. Present small units at a time. If a pre-reading discussion is necessary, do this first.

- Read aloud, having the pupil follow along.
- Summarize what you have read. Point out important details and paraphrase in a way that helps the pupil to understand the main idea of the reading.
- Clarify anything you don't understand: unfamiliar vocabulary, new or difficult concepts, when you might have lost track of the meaning or found the structure difficult. Some strategies that may restore meaning are: rereading, looking up words in the dictionary/ thesaurus or discussing phrases which may be unfamiliar, confusing or difficult to understand.
- Ask questions about what you have read. This stage could lead to additional questions and result in a dialogue by offering possible solutions or providing relevant information.
- Make a prediction about what will happen next. This will provoke imagination and can also provide an opportunity for the pupils critically to assess the author's intent. This also provides a purpose for continuing to read as further reading will confirm or reject their prediction.

Now the pupil takes a turn, repeating the same process. Eventually the pupil will learn to go through this process without the support of the teacher. However, this technique takes a lot of modelling and practising.

MAPPING AND WEBBING

Have the pupil create a map as they are reading to use as a reference when recapping or answering comprehension questions. The map is their own personal account of the information they are reading, so they should be able to do it in their own style. In that way they will remember the information better and make sense of it when they refer to it later.

The map will also serve as a visual aid for keeping track of what they have read.

There are many options for creating maps, depending on the reading and the task. You can use a pre-made map or web with headings and subheadings to begin with and then graduate to having the pupil organize one himself. The map can be a sequential plan of a story to make the sequence easier to follow or it can be a detailed account of the main points of a book. For example, a character web could be used for a description of the main character, such as Anne Frank. This can be added to when the pupil comes across a detail from the story, as going back later and looking for the details can be a difficult task.

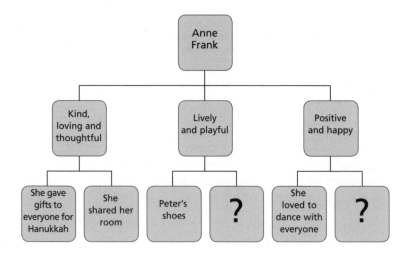

Charts and other visual aids can help to highlight the bigger picture and provide a visual overview of a topic. They can be used to show anything, from the life cycle of a butterfly to a timeline of historical events. The important point is that the chart is visually appealing as this makes it easier for the dyslexic learner to follow and understand.

It is a good idea to get the pupils to make their own chart, or visual aid, but they may have to obtain an overview of the text first before they can do a chart showing the key events. If charts are being provided, ensure that they are clearly labelled, with bold type used for any arrows or lines.

You can use a chart in history when sequencing dates and events. This can be made into a timeline that, for example, chronicles the dates of a king's reign, the passing of the laws of the country, the development of towns or ports, or a week in the life of a nine-year-old boy in the nineteenth century. Some colour can be added to the timeline to show different periods or different types of events. For example, if doing a timeline on the reign of kings and queens all the wars can be in red, the births in blue and the marriages in green.

A timeline can also provide the pupil with an opportunity to practise writing a 'key' for added meaning, helping to interpret the symbols on the page. A 'key' can be a difficult concept for a dyslexic child to understand so it is good to take the opportunity to practise using this.

Timeline		
Symbol or graphic	**Date**	**Event**

CHARTS, TIMELINES

'SOAP' GESTURE

Gestures are important as they demonstrate emotions and feelings and this can enhance and facilitate comprehension of the text.

A good homework/class follow-up exercise is to compile a list of everyday emotions such as happy, afraid, angry, disappointed, worried. Get the pupils to watch a TV programme – suggest one of the children's 'soap' programmes. The pupils have to tick off the gesture from their list when they see it being used. They then have to make up an appropriate sentence which they can use with each gesture. They can also do the gesture to the class and the pupils who have watched the same programme have to try to work out which part of the TV programme the gesture describes.

This emphasizes that comprehension is more than just reading because it also involves non-verbal communication. As an alternative, get pupils to make a list of the gestures and cut them into strips – one strip for each gesture – and put them into a bucket. Each person has to pick one out and act out that gesture, while the others in the class have to say which gesture is being used and which part of the TV programme it refers to. This is a good interactive class activity. The class can follow this up by drawing each of the gestures.

This can be an excellent activity for dyslexic learners as they are able to hear the story and can also follow it in print at the same time. It can also help with word recognition, as well as providing important language experience.

Select some texts that the child is able to read fluently and record the child reading them (taping should be done in stages). This allows the child to hear his own voice reading a piece of text fluently, which develops self-confidence. Then move on to some texts the child has difficulty reading – when you are recording these share the reading with an adult, certainly to begin with, as in paired reading (see Idea 61). Gradually allow the child to do most of the recording himself. It is also important to discuss the text with the child at this point to help develop comprehension. Remember to keep the tapes as a record of the child's progress and use them to demonstrate this progress to the child himself.

Getting it taped checklist				
Process	**Text**	**Parts taped**	**Dates listened**	**Self-test carried out**
1. **Text selected with child's comfort zone**				
2. **Recorded**				
3. **Made available to the child**				
4. **Challenging texts taped**				
5. **Child does recording**				
6. **Comprehension activities carried out**				

It is important to ensure that the child is involved in the story, or the factual information, when reading new text. This can apply to a class reader, a novel or a textbook. The best way to do this is to help him gain maximum understanding from the text as early as possible in the reading activity.

Before reading the text, ask him what he understands by the title. This can give some indication of the pupil's background understanding. Some of the questions that can be asked after a short period of reading a novel, for example, include: Are you enjoying the story and why/why not? Who are the main characters and how do you know that? Then ask the pupil to make predictions about what might happen next and some likely endings to the story.

It is also important to ensure that you recognize the different levels of understanding, whether it is a novel/story or factual/information-type text. These levels shown below are important because they go further than a basic understanding and can encourage reflection and help the reader to become more involved in the text.

- Literal level – factual information such as who, why, how was that done?
- Inferential level – the inferences, or 'reading between the lines'. This includes questions such as: What do you think will happen next? Why do you think he said that?
- Creative level – this encourages originality and reflection. Tasks such as write (or say) a different ending to the story can develop this level of understanding.
- Critical level – this encourages reflection. Questions that can help with this level include: Did you enjoy the book – why? What was confusing about the book? Was the plot easy to follow – why/why not?

These levels could also apply to factual texts, particularly the critical level. It is important to encourage dyslexic pupils to think critically when accessing text as it encourages the view that reading is not only about accuracy but also about gaining meaning from text.

Many young people with dyslexia have difficulty writing about what they have read, although they may have a picture in their mind. If they create a visual record of the main idea of each chapter they can use the pictures as a prompt when they are retelling the story. It can be a great way to keep a record of the sequence of events.

After reading a chapter, have the pupil close his eyes and ask him to form a picture in his mind of what the chapter was about. Discuss what he is visualizing to ensure he is on track. Then ask the pupil to draw a picture of what he sees – do this on a card and write the chapter number in the top right-hand corner. He does not have to be an artist – stick figures work just as well. Add a splash of colour if time permits. If it is a longer chapter, the pupil could do several drawings taken from the beginning, middle and end of the chapter. This can help with the sequencing of the action in the chapter. When he has finished with the book the pupil will have a visual, sequential record of what the reading was about and can then use the visuals as triggers when he is required to retell the story.

It is also an idea to visualize and draw the main characters. The pupil should try to show the main features described by the author; for example, a long pointed nose, short or long, dark or light hair. These features could be drawn in an exaggerated fashion.

There is no writing or note-taking in this idea, although the next step would be for the pupil to summarize in writing what he has drawn.

PICTURE THIS!

SEQUENCING EVENTS

For those dyslexic pupils who struggle with sequencing it is important that they keep a record of the sequence of events. This should be very brief, just outlining the main events, and could also be done in bullet point form. Pupils can use this sequence of events when they are recapping the story/event orally.

Title: _____

Author: _____

Sequence of events

Chapter 1 _____

_____

_____

_____

_____

_____

_____

Chapter 2 _____

_____

_____

_____

_____

_____

Some pupils may prefer to write notes on each chapter on a record card and combine it with visuals (see Idea 72).

Encouraging sentence expansion is important for dyslexic pupils as it helps to develop expressive writing. This can be practised by taking vocabulary from the pupils' readers and using these words to develop sentence writing.

Obtain a selection of vocabulary from a book the pupil is familiar with and make up some phrases using this vocabulary. Then get the pupil to put these phrases into sentences. Decide on new vocabulary (target vocabulary) that can connect to these phrases, and the pupil then has to make up new phrases using this new target vocabulary. Next, these phrases can be joined together into more complex sentences.

Encourage the pupil to illustrate some of the sentences, helping to give them a specific meaning. As well as developing sentence expansion this can also help with creative writing.

This is a great opportunity to teach children about different types of phrases. To teach about prepositional phrases you must first teach what prepositions, nouns and adjectives are. For example, prepositions tell us 'where' something is or 'when' something is happening. A prepositional phrase will begin with a preposition and end with a noun. You may have an adjective before the noun. Ask students to draw a tree in the centre of their page. Next ask them to write down phrases that will tell you where in relation to the tree they can be:

under the tree
behind the tree
on the branch
in front of the tree
beside the tree.

Next create a list of when they were there:

after lunch
before dinner.

Now have the students incorporate prepositional phrases into their sentences thereby expanding the sentence and making it more interesting.

It is important for children with dyslexia to obtain practice at reading in order to improve reading fluency. One way of working on fluency is to reread books they are familiar with. It is preferable to develop a sequence for this activity and to adopt a planned procedure.

Begin with children selecting some books they like, are familiar with and are able to read reasonably well. Then ask them to select one book at a time and to tell you, or write down, what they think the book is about. It is important to ask them to find new information or details about the book that they have not previously written about. Each time they read they have to find some new information about the book. This activity can be done using a chart with the key characters/events outlined. They can then write something new about the characters and the events each time they read the book. It is possible to time the reading and try to encourage them to read in a shorter time, thereby also increasing reading fluency.

Dyslexic pupils often have difficulty with reading accuracy but can develop good comprehension. They will read for meaning rather than accuracy, making mistakes when reading aloud, but still gaining a good level of comprehension of the text. It is important to encourage reading methods that can improve comprehension and help them identify the key words in a passage. But it is also necessary to show them strategies that highlight the different purposes of reading. For that reason, try to provide the pupil with descriptions of different kinds of reading techniques and how and when they can be used. Some examples are shown below:

Skimming – reading only the main headings, introduction and conclusion. Use skimming to check whether you want to read more of the text.

Scanning – looking for a particular key word or phrase. Before you start scanning, 'see' the word or phrase in your mind, then look quickly down the page. Try to focus on the middle of each line as your eye moves down the page.

Reading for pleasure – you may want to use more visual imagery, reading as a means of escape. You should be relaxed when you do this.

Reading for detail – reading every word very carefully and even rereading some words or sentences to ensure you get the meaning accurately. You are focusing here on accuracy.

Once the pupils understand this, provide them with some examples of types of reading and get them to choose the appropriate technique, placing them under the right heading. You could use symbols for each reading technique to give the exercise a visual feel.

Technique	Task	Comment
Skimming		
Scanning		
Reading for pleasure		
Reading for detail		

Provide the student with some tasks and get them to insert these into the appropriate box above.

Tasks

- Find a date in history (skimming)
- Making notes for an essay
- Deciding which chapter is the main one in a book
- Reading a novel
- Reading a newspaper article
- Reading a magazine
- Doing a timeline for history
- Reading a mathematics problem.

It is useful to ask the student to comment on the task – for example, he may write down the aspects he found challenging and what he may need to work more on.

It is important to informally check the level of the text to ensure it is appropriate for learners with dyslexia. The readability of a text refers to the ease of reading and understanding. There are formal and precise procedures that can be used for assessing readability levels and some publishers list the reading level on the back of the book. However, these numbers can be confusing and some publishers are seen to be either notoriously high or low in predicting the reading level. This is usually because the publishers are looking at different criteria to judge the reading level. For example, some may look at vocabulary and length while others will look at content, style and plot. It can be useful to carry out some informal practices that can help to pinpoint the readability of the text for the child you are working with.

You should consider the following for informal assessment of readability level:

1. Size of the type. You may want to go for larger font sizes. This helps the reader focus more on the shape and structure of letters, words and the sentences.
2. Number of words in a sentence. You should select a text with shorter sentences if the child's reading level is low.
3. Number of syllables in the words. One- or two-syllable words are good for early readers, and compound words and those with suffixes and prefixes become more common as reading level raises.
4. Check the style as well as any unusual punctuation or grammatical features.
5. The narrative – this is important – if the plot is too complex the child with dyslexia may not be able to comprehend it to begin with.
6. Count the number of errors the child makes as they begin reading a chapter in a book. If you reach five errors before the child reaches the end of the first page, it is likely too difficult.

PROVIDING BACKGROUND VOCABULARY, DISCUSSION AND STRUCTURE

Many dyslexic pupils enjoy English literature but often find the background vocabulary in some novels demanding. It is important that they are able to appreciate and interpret novels and therefore it is a good idea to provide this background vocabulary before they start on the novel study. This will include putting the vocabulary in context and therefore introducing any new themes that will come up in the novel. There are several ways to present the vocabulary but what is important for the dyslexic learner is that it is presented in a multisensory way and that the student keeps a record of the vocabulary to refer back to. This could be in the form of a personal dictionary or on index cards that can be kept in a box or bound together. The vocabulary should be presented clearly and explicitly. This is a teaching step and not a guessing game for the student. The student could look words up in a dictionary or in a reference book. Then discuss the meaning of the word with the student, provide graphics if possible and then have the student record the meaning. It is also very helpful to use the word in a phrase, taken directly from the novel. These could be written on index cards and the student can work through the list, looking words up, discussing the meaning in context of the phrase and then recording it. It is also a possibility to have the student draw a picture that represents the word in their personal dictionary. This will help them recall the meaning as it makes it more personal.

This can be a time consuming exercise but the advantages for the student can make a huge difference for reading fluency and reading comprehension. When they come to these words in the novel, they will hopefully be familiar and therefore will not have to stop to sound out or look a word up. The idea is that their fluency and comprehension will not be compromised by words they don't understand or can't pronounce.

Creative writing

KWL GRIDS

KWL Grids are well established graphical organizers designed to help in learning. They were originally created by Donna Ogle in 1986. It is a simple but effective way of scaffolding to support children doing research and recording learning in many areas of the curriculum.

The KWL Grids are made up of three columns and are completely student centred.

The first column, K, asks the child to write 'What they already **K**now' about a subject or topic. This stimulates prior experiences or background knowledge about the topic to be studied. They may need help with this first step so have questions prepared ahead of time that will stimulate their thinking. They may brainstorm words, phrases, sentences or stories about the topic.

The next column, W, asks the child to write 'What they **W**ant to Know' about the topic to be studied. This step establishes a purpose and should be completed before reading of the text to be studied.

The third column is to be completed after reading the text or passage and asks the child to record what they have learned about the topic.

KWL Grids can be used as a whole-class activity, in small groups or individually. The teacher can scribe or the children can record information independently. For this activity to be most effective, it should be modelled by the teacher so the children are familiar with the process before the children attempt it independently.

K	W	L
'What I Know'	'What I Want to Know'	'What I have Learned'

The objective in a creative writing project is to get the pupils to write. However, this doesn't have to be the physical act of writing. Many dyslexic pupils have fabulous ideas but they can't get them down on paper because of their difficulties with writing. In this case it may be necessary to provide a scribe for the pupil, not just for exams but for writing projects.

Scribing is a way of helping the pupil produce a text of his own. The scribe can be the teacher, tutor, parent or a classmate. The key is to write down what the pupil says, not what you think he should say, and read it back to him so that he can hear it, and then let him make any changes. The goal is to produce a piece of written material that conveys what the pupil wants it to.

There are many ways to do this without affecting the pupil's self-esteem. In a classroom you could put the pupils into pairs or groups and have one pupil do the writing. If you are working in a one-to-one situation already, then simply tell the pupil you will scribe as you just want him to think and not be distracted by a pen and paper.

A pupil may need someone to scribe for them if they have:

- dysgraphia – difficulty with handwriting and motor control that can affect handwriting and pencil grip
- difficulties with spelling and grammar
- poor written output – often dyslexic pupils can be good orally but have a difficulty in displaying this in written form
- problems with pencil grip and handwriting fatigue.

(Idea 83 can be used as an activity to determine whether or not a pupil would improve their writing with a scribe.)

BRAINSTORMING

Brainstorming is a great way for pupils to develop their vocabulary and to get them thinking more quickly. When they are finished with a brainstorming activity, they will have a list of ideas to work from for writing. Try to get the pupils to write a good long list of at least ten or more items.

It is important to note that spelling never counts in brainstorming activities and it is often a good idea to have someone scribing (see Idea 80) so that the pupil can just focus on getting the ideas out. Try to vary the activities by using a whiteboard or a chalkboard to get away from a regular lined piece of paper and pencil. You may also let the pupils stand and toss a Koosh ball or hacky sack (something that doesn't bounce) back and forth as not all of them will think best when they are sitting at a desk.

Choose a topic to brainstorm that will be of some interest to your pupils, as follows:

- Skateboard brand names
- Vacation destinations
- Things that are green
- Sports equipment
- Things to take to the beach
- Cars
- Types of dogs
- Musicians
- Favourite snack foods
- Music concert
- Football game
- My favourite weekend
- Summer holiday
- Carnival hits the town
- Train journey
- Snow.

Mapping is a great way to organize ideas for a writing project.

Have the pupils brainstorm a list of their ten favourite things, then ask them to number the list from one to ten, with one being their absolute favourite. Give the pupils a blank sheet of paper and ask them to draw a cloud or circle in the centre of the page. Inside this they write 'My favourite things'. Next they must write their three top favourite things coming out from the centre like a web, and sketch a small drawing of each thing.

The next step is getting the pupils to expand on each of their favourite things with details and descriptive words – the 'what' and 'why' of their favourite things. They should also continue adding visuals that represent what they are writing. Putting in a bit of colour will help with the detail and the description when they move on to the paragraph writing stage.

For example, one of their favourite things might be rain:

My favourite things

Rain

- Feels good on my skin
  - Tingly
  - Cold
  - Wet
  - Taste (catching raindrops on my tongue)

- Smell
  - Fresh
  - Damp

- Sound
  - Loud thunder
  - Rain on rooftops.

Once the pupils are finished with their webs they can develop them into an introductory paragraph, a paragraph for each of their favourite things and then a concluding paragraph. One of the keys to success with this activity is to develop it slowly, without telling the pupils that the final goal is to write several paragraphs. Just give them the small steps, one at a time.

VISUALS

Giving a pupil a visual image to write about is a great way to stimulate ideas. Choose a picture that will be interesting to the pupil and will provoke a discussion. Allow 2 or 3 minutes for the pupil to study the picture and then ask him to tell you what he sees. Remember that this is an activity to stimulate imagination and he may see something you didn't think of, or his ideas may take him in a different direction to that which you had in mind.

Be prepared with three questions about the picture to ask the pupil in case you get an answer of 'I don't know', and ensure that the questions are open ended so that he can't simply answer with a yes or no.

Keep your goal in mind during the discussion – is this going to be a descriptive paragraph or a narrative? The discussion should involve details and prepare the pupil to write a paragraph (or more) about the picture.

The picture could show:

- people with interesting facial expressions
- animals
- sports
- a beach scene
- interesting activities
- cartoon images.

Once the discussion is complete, give the pupil paper and a writing tool to write his paragraph. It will be interesting to note the difference between what the pupil is able to tell you during the discussion compared with what he is able to write. (This is a good activity to do when trying to determine whether a pupil needs someone to scribe for him when writing – see Idea 80.)

DRAW A FOREST

Pupils with dyslexia often freeze up when they are asked to write as it can be such a daunting task for them. If they are given a creative way to express their ideas and thoughts which then slowly leads into a writing exercise they can be much more successful.

This exercise should be taken in small steps which lead up to the final written piece. It can be particularly good for those pupils who like to draw, but it isn't necessary to be an artist to have success.

The first step is to build up some forest vocabulary. Talk about the kind of things you might find in a forest and encourage the pupils to use a thesaurus to develop their vocabulary further.

Give the pupils a large piece of paper each and have them draw the outline of a forest – it can be any shape they like. Draw in the detail:

- Are there hills or mountains?
- Is there a shoreline – are there beaches or is the forest at the edge of a steep cliff? Do the beaches have sand or rocks?
- Are there streams and rivers? Are they wide and lazy or dangerous, with white water rapids?
- What about lakes, swamps or marshes?
- Is it sunny or does it rain all the time?
- What kind of trees are in the forest?
- What sorts of insects, reptiles, birds or mammals live in the forest?
- What do you smell?
- How does the air feel?

Encourage them to add colour to their forest drawing. When they have completed their drawing they can organize their ideas and write several paragraphs describing their forest.

FOREST ADVENTURE

Building on the idea of drawing a forest in Idea 84, you can now use the drawing as inspiration for writing an adventure story that takes place in the forest.

With their drawings in front of them on their desks, say to the pupils something along the lines of: 'You want to visit your forest, so how are you going to get there? Can you fly, is there a place to land a plane or do you need to take a helicopter? Do you need to take a boat or maybe a floatplane? Can you hike, ride a bike, ride a horse or drive in a jeep? You see a path, take a step and you are in your forest! Keep walking but think about how you are going to keep track of where you are and where you are going. Suddenly there is a turn in the path – who or what do you encounter? Are you worried, scared, excited, apprehensive or anxious?'

Ask the pupils to write down key words that describe their adventure. They can make a list of how they are feeling, what they see and what they do on their walk through the forest. They may choose to encounter obstacles, creatures or people who may be make-believe or real. This is their adventure and they should have fun with it.

Following the forest theme of the two previous ideas, you could get your pupils to send a postcard from their forest. Ask them to decide who they are going to send it to and to think about what they want to say. Are they in trouble and needing help? Are they having a wonderful time and wanting to tell of their adventures? Are they inviting someone to visit their forest?

They should write a rough draft and then write their good copy on a provided outline of a postcard. On the front they could draw a smaller picture of their forest or some aspect of it, such as an animal or tree found there. You could give them a small, square piece of paper for their postage stamp and they could draw a visual of their forest on it and fill in the correct postage amount.

When the pupils have completed their postcards they can exchange them with another pupil or send them home to a parent or grandparent.

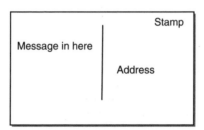

POSTCARDS

IDEA
87

COLLAGE

A good way to stimulate creative writing is to get pupils to go through magazines and cut out interesting pictures (at least six) based on a theme. The theme may be sports, a beach scene or it could simply be interesting people. The pupils then create a collage by gluing their pictures onto a sheet of coloured paper. This can be used for writing either a narrative, descriptive or compare-and-contrast paragraph. The type of paragraph will depend on the pictures and the theme chosen.

Before the pupils start to write, they should brainstorm a list of describing words based on the collage. These can then be put into a web to help the pupils organize their ideas.

Preparation for a collage – brainstorming and organizing information

Put an object into a bag that is not transparent. If you are doing this activity with a class, organize the class into pairs and have each pupil choose an object to put into a bag for a partner, without showing the other pupils. Ask them to exchange bags.

The pupils then reach into the bag, without looking, and feel the object. Each pupil has to come up with a list of words describing the object (at least four words, more if possible). They then have to write a paragraph describing the object and end with a sentence saying what they think the object is. These can be read aloud to the class or to their partners. The object is taken out of the bag and the pupils can see if their guesses were correct.

It will be helpful to provide a writing frame for this activity such as the one below.

_____   _____
_____   _____
_____   _____
_____
_____
_____
_____
_____

_____

I think the object is

_____

A Diamanté-style poem provides an opportunity to create a complete composition with little guidance and prompting. Diamanté poems are a wonderful tool for incorporating the pupil's knowledge of nouns, verbs and adjectives while building vocabulary and triggering the imagination. The poem is arranged in a diamond pattern using seven lines. For example:

——

—— ——

—— —— ——

—— —— —— ——

—— —— ——

—— ——

——

- Line 1 – one word (subject/noun)
- Line 2 – two words (adjectives)
- Line 3 – three words (-ing verbs)
- Line 4 – four words (nouns)
- Line 5 – three words (-ing verbs)
- Line 6 – two words (adjectives)
- Line 7 – one word (noun)

To prepare for this activity on, for example, a beach theme:

- Teach the parts of speech (nouns, adjectives, verbs)
- Read a beach story
- Discuss a day at the beach – each pupil can tell the group a story about the beach or a favourite beach experience they have had
- Ask pupils to draw a picture of the beach (have beach pictures ready to show)
- Pupils choose nouns, verbs and adjectives to describe their pictures
- The poem should be written in rough and then a good copy produced to accompany the drawing
- Pictures can be drawn around the poem.

Spelling

Spelling can be a daunting task for dyslexic pupils as the English language has a number of complexities. It is important that spelling rules and the irregular aspects of the language are taught so that pupils can use their skills to stop and think about which rules or concepts can be applied to the word they are spelling. This way they can use their cognitive abilities to make the best possible choice. If pupils who struggle with spelling are taught the spelling rules explicitly and have plenty of opportunities to practise them, many common spelling errors can be eliminated.

An example of teaching the 'Final e rule' is shown below. Words ending in an 'e':

- Drop the 'e' before a suffix beginning with a vowel – late + er = later
- Keep the 'e' if the suffix begins with a consonant – late + ly = lately

Word	Suffix	Beginning with a vowel or a consonant?	Drop the 'e' or keep the 'e'?	New word
gate	-ed	v	drop	gated
grate	-ful	c	keep	grateful
like	-ly			
hope	-ing			
spite	-ful			

Every spelling rule has exceptions, but these should not be introduced until the concepts are secure otherwise they may cause confusion.

Exceptions to the 'Final e rule':

- Keep the 'e' to protect a soft 'c' or a soft 'g' (courageous, serviceable, peaceable)
- Keep the 'e' to protect the meaning of a word (singeing, dyeing, acreage).

The difficulty with teaching spelling rules is that often the pupils have trouble remembering them. One way to support them in remembering the rule is to allow them to have a code representing the spelling rule or concept being taught. You could use a code for the doubling rule (if you have a one-syllable word, with one short vowel, ending in one consonant, double the final consonant if the suffix begins with a vowel – for example, run, running), such as:

S = syllable; v = vowel;
c = consonant; sf = suffix

```
1s 1v 1c
   cc
  sf-v
```

Teach the vocabulary:

- Syllable: a syllable is a word or a part of a word with one vowel sound – run
- Short vowel: 'a' as in apple, 'e' as in Ed, 'i' as in insect, 'o' as in hop and 'u' as in up
- Consonant: any letter that is not a vowel
- Suffix: a unit added to the end of a word that has meaning and changes the meaning of a word. For example, -ed, -ing, -er.

Teach specific suffixes that pupils will need to use the rule, such as -ing, -ed, -er, -est, -ment, -ness. Use this table to practise the rules.

Word + suffix	1 syllable	1 short vowel	Ends in 1 consonant	Suffix begins with a vowel	Double?	Spelling
run + -ing	yes	yes	yes	yes	yes	running
bump + -ed	yes	yes	no	yes	no	bumped
hop + -er	yes	yes	yes	yes	yes	hopper
fun + -y						
smug + -ness						
Plan + -ed						

Codes can be developed for all the spelling rules and concepts and used as a memory trigger for pupils, but keep them simple – the less the pupil has to remember the better. Allow pupils to use a code card when spelling, even during tests, until spelling becomes automatic.

Block spelling is beneficial for pupils who tend to leave out letters, put letters in the wrong place or add in extra ones. It is most suitable for one-syllable words.

Give the pupil more markers (use beads, blocks, bingo chips, happy faces) than are in the word. The pupil then says the word, pushing one marker forward for each sound. He then knows how many sounds need to be represented when he is spelling. Begin with consonant vowel consonant (cvc) words and add beginning and final blends as the pupil is able to spell with more phonograms (letters or groups of letters representing one sound) (ccvcc).

For example, 'blast'. Dictate the word blast, the pupil repeats the word and then pushes a marker forward for each sound his mouth says.

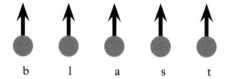

b	l	a	s	t

The pupil says aloud the sound of each phonogram, it is not written for them.

Looking at the circles, he will know that when he spells blast, he will need to have five letters on his paper. For pupils who struggle with vowels, use a different colour to represent the vowel.

b	l	a	s	t

Eventually he will know that when he hears 'ch' he will need one marker (one sound) and that sound is spelled with either 'ch' or 'tch'. These concepts need to be carefully taught before using them in block spelling.

Pupils often have more success if they can associate a visual with a new or troublesome phonogram. For example, the sound 's' can be formed into the shape of a snake. You could have the pupil draw a picture of or colour a picture of a snake in the form of an 's'.

Often the short vowel sounds are difficult for pupils to discriminate. Giving them a key word and a visual can be a great aid. For example, if the short vowel sounds for 'e' and 'i' are causing difficulties for a pupil, use a visual of a boy named Ed and a visual of an insect. You can also give kinaesthetic clues (relating to active experiences) such as 'Insects make me itchy', and 'Scratch in an up and down motion like an "i".' From that point forward, every time the pupil is unsure of the vowel sound you can give him the key word or the kinaesthetic clue. When he is working independently he can match the sound in his key words to the sound in the word he is spelling. In this way the learning is cognitive – the pupil must stop and think about what the correct spelling is for the sound.

You could let pupils choose their own key words and visuals or develop your own.

Get the student to keep a chart of the phonograms, key words and the visuals used to remember it. Another option would be to use index cards with the phonogram on one side and the key word and visual on the back.

Phonogram	Key word	Visual
i	insect	

SOUND AS YOU SPELL

Often when pupils are spelling they insert extra letters, leave letters out, confuse vowel sounds or put letters in the wrong place. They may spell 'felt' for 'left' – all the letters are correct, but not in the right order. They may confuse the short vowel sounds by spelling 'blemp' for 'blimp' or they may leave out letters as in 'spash' for 'splash'.

If pupils sound the word as they are spelling it, they are more likely to spell the word correctly so long as they have the phonetic skills to do so. Initially, they can sound out loud as they are spelling and then when they are more comfortable with the process, they can sound as they spell silently. When teaching this technique be sure to demonstrate on a whiteboard that your hand will spell what your mouth says.

If pupils use this process at the start of their spelling journey they will begin with consonant vowel consonant (cvc as in run) and then move to ccvc (as in stun) which will include the use of common beginning blends such as 'sp', 'st' or 'gl'. The next step is to add final blends such as 'mp', 'nd' and 'xt' (ccvcc as in stump). Eventually they will be able to sound as they spell with digraphs ('sh', 'ch', 'th'), diphthongs ('oi', 'ou') and multiple spelling choices ('o', 'oa', 'ow').

One way to remind pupils to 'sound as they spell' is to have a visual of a mouth and another of a hand holding a pencil.

A multiple spelling choice occurs when a pupil hears a sound and must choose between more than one spelling for that sound; for example, the sound 'ch' can be spelled with a 'ch' or with 'tch'. If the pupil hears a short vowel sound immediately before the 'ch' sound he will know that the sound he is spelling will be 'tch' as in latch.

Develop word charts for multiple spelling choices. In each word chart give the multiple spelling, the concept behind each spelling, and an example of a word using that spelling with a visual of that word. Then randomly dictate words with those multiple spelling choices. Each word should contain one of the spellings. For example:

oa	**ow**
Use a visual of a boat here	Use a visual of snow here
boat	snow
middle spelling	final spelling
_____	_____
_____	_____
_____	_____
_____	_____

Be sure that pupils are confident in using each individual phonogram before introducing a multiple spelling choice. For example, only introduce 'ow' as in snow when you are certain 'oa' for boat is secure. Then the pupils can be given words with both spellings and asked to stop and think about which one they are going to use – 'ow', as in snow, is a final spelling and 'oa', as in boat, is a middle (or beginning) spelling.

WORD LISTS

Dyslexic pupils struggle with spelling high-frequency words and so compromise their writing because they don't know how to spell a word they want to use. Providing a word list, made up of high-frequency words, will help them overcome some of these spelling difficulties. The pupil can then refer to the list for the spelling of any words of which he is unsure.

Word lists can be quite general, composed of words commonly used by pupils at certain ages. They can also be in the form of specific lists focusing on the pupil's own particular spelling difficulties. The list below shows some common words for Year 2 pupils.

Other word lists can be made up for different subject areas and are especially useful for subjects which involve learning a considerable amount of specialized and technical vocabulary.

I	to	it	he	one
and	my	went	on	she
the	was	in	said	day
a	is	there	they	we
home	with	dad	so	of
me	like	had	were	at

Pupils who struggle with spelling need to be given strategies for reviewing and learning the spelling of words. The following strategy may be helpful in memorizing word patterns and words which cannot be sounded out.

Look – this involves the active engagement of the writer, who looks closely at the word with the intention of reproducing it. It is important that this stage is not skipped or rushed through before the pupil has had an opportunity to develop visual strategies to help memorize the visual features of the word. These can include tracing the word with a finger, looking for shapes and patterns and any distinctive features, comparing the visual features and similarities of the letters and the word to other words. For example, in the word 'window' there are a number of visual aspects which could help with memory, such as the first and last letter being the same and the distinctiveness of the letter 'w'. At this stage it is also possible to draw attention to words within words, such as tent in attention and ask in basket.

Cover – this involves covering the word and also helps strengthen the visual memory.

Write – this is an important stage as it provides the pupil with kinaesthetic practice. At this stage, cursive handwriting is often encouraged and there may well be a link between clear cursive writing and good spelling.

Check – this provides the dyslexic learner with some responsibility for his own spelling. It is important to reduce the dependency on the teacher as soon as possible and to promote self-correction.

LOOK, COVER, WRITE, CHECK

Dyslexic pupils often need to be taught in a multisensory way. This means that they will have more success if spelling is taught and reinforced using visual, auditory, tactile and kinaesthetic strategies. Simultaneous Oral Spelling, suggested by Lynette Bradley, is a strategy that encompasses all of these. Ask the pupil to:

- look at the word written correctly, or made with tactile letters
- say the word
- write the word, sounding out each phonogram as it is written (it is best to use a cursive script). As the pupil writes he must look at each letter and hear its sound. He will receive kinaesthetic feedback through the movement of the arm and throat muscles
- check to see if the word is correct
- cover up the word and repeat the process. Continue to practise the word in this way, three times a day, for one week. By this time the word should be committed to memory. However, only one word will have been learned.

The final step involves the categorization of the word with other words which sound and look alike. So if the word that has been learnt is 'round', the pupil is then shown that he can also spell ground, pound, found, mound, sound, around, bound, grounded, pounding, and so on. He has learned eight or more words for the effort of learning one.

Visualizing the word can be a successful strategy for some dyslexic pupils. This process involves the following:

- Look at the word
- Cover the word with a piece of paper
- Try to see the word – visualize it – on the paper
- Copy the word as you see it
- Check to see if you have spelt the word correctly
- Have a ten-minute break and then repeat the exercise
- A few hours later repeat this again
- Then repeat this at various times over the next few days
- Add a new word to the list each week and repeat the above sequence.

VISUALIZATION

Practice visualization and association – word and visual

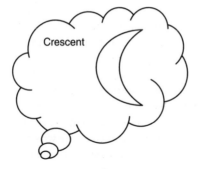

Crescent

IDEA

100

Cued Spelling is a simple yet effective technique that shares the same principles as paired reading (see Idea 61). Cued Spelling developed originally by Keith Topping (www.pre-online.co.uk/feature_pdfs/spotlight82.pdf) comprises the following ten steps:

1. Pupils selected a word to learn or were given target words
2. Pairs entered the words into their spelling diaries
3. Pairs read the word together
4. Speller and helper choose cue together
5. Pairs repeat cues aloud
6. Speller says cues while helper writes word
7. Helper says cues while speller writes word
8. Speller writes word quickly and says cues aloud
9. Speller writes word quickly
10. Speller reads word aloud.

The technique also includes daily reviews where the pupil writes all the words for the day and checks them – the wrong words are then noted and the learner goes through the ten steps again for these words. The pupil adopts the same procedure for the weekly review and identifies the wrong words. Discussion would then take place on the best approach for the learner to tackle the wrongly spelt words. If the learner writes a word inaccurately he is encouraged to delete the word from memory by erasing it or boldly scoring it out. This can be particularly useful if the pupil has a strong visual memory and the image of the incorrect word may remain and be recalled at some future point. The cued spelling technique is highly interactive and attempts to eliminate the fear of failure through the use of prompt correction procedures.

Syllabication is the practice of dividing words into syllables. Syllables are made up a single vowel sound with or without a consonant sound or sounds. The vowel sound may be made up by more than one vowel but there is only one sound as in the word rain. Rain is one syllable with the 'ai' working together to make the long /a/ sound. All words consist of at least one syllable. The word 'I' has one vowel sound and is one syllable. The word 'bread' has one vowel sound and is one syllable and the word 'idea' has three distinct vowel sounds and is three syllables.

Learning to read and spell according to syllables is a natural progression from analyzing words sound by sound. Recognizing syllables will ease the spelling and reading of polysyllabic words.

Teaching syllabication should be a process moving from simple to the more complex skills.

1. Teach what a syllable is: 'A syllable is a word or a part of a word with one vowel sound'. Breaking words into syllables is first taught as a phonological awareness skill without too much concern over exactly where the syllable divides. In other words the concern should be over ensuring there is a vowel sound in each syllable. At this stage there should not be any grapheme representation. Show graphics of the word but the child should only hear the word, not see it.

2. Practice counting syllables with words containing one, two, three, four or more syllables: The child does not need to read or spell these words. They hear the word, repeat the word and count the syllables. Clapping out the syllables is a good way to begin but it is easier to keep track of the number of syllables if you use counters. You can use smalls rocks, beads, shells, bingo chips, paper clips or anything else you have in the classroom.

SYLLABICATION

3. Teach the type of syllable: There are six different syllable types and these should be taught individually and then practised before moving to the next one.
4. Teach how to divide between different types of syllables: Practise dividing words and identifying the type of syllable in each division.

Number work/maths

IDEA
102

Dyslexic pupils have difficulty with abstract mathematical concepts. It is necessary to use concrete examples to explain new concepts or even simple mathematical problems. This also applies to multiplication and addition.

Use real money or plastic/paper money when doing additions and subtractions. Allow the dyslexic child to use his fingers and use blocks and beads and other concrete articles so he can touch and move them around. Some children may actually need to draw the shape of the numbers with their fingers in the air.

The important point to remember is that dyslexic children tend to have a preference for a visual, kinaesthetic and random processing style. This means they will need visual and concrete learning aids and will have difficulty in following sequences – that is why it is an idea to allow them to work out problems in a random style as long as it suits their own individual preference. It is also useful to ensure they articulate the process they are going through and, if possible, jot it down so they can go back over their steps if they make a mistake.

Mathematics can be a subject that is governed by rules and formulae. Often this involves linear and sequential processing. These are aspects of the learning process that can be very challenging for dyslexic pupils. It is important, therefore, that they are able to use their strengths and their own strategies to do this. They will develop their own interrelationships and methods for doing problems and, with practice, can become effective at using these strategies. But it is important that they are able to recognize how they tackle problems involving numbers.

Provide a series of arithmetical problems – addition, subtraction, multiplication and division. Ask the pupils to write down how they obtained an answer to a particular problem. If they have difficulty in writing it down they can tell you orally.

Give them problems that are known to be demanding or confusing for dyslexic pupils.

These can include sums such as $8 + 7$. Many dyslexic people will do this by working out $8 + 8$ less 1. Another one is 4×7 which can be derived from $2 \times 7 \times 2$. It is important that they write down how they arrived at the answer, even if the answer is incorrect. You can also provide some multiplication and division using single and double numbers. Get them to note the steps they are taking in solving more complex problems. They need to be aware of these steps, and simpler activities such as the one above can help them with this.

ENCOURAGING THEIR OWN STRATEGIES AND LEARNING STYLE

Software can allow the pupil to work independently, but make sure that the software:

- is flexible so that the pupil can move easily around the program
- gives the pupil choice – voice output or graphics
- has clear voice output
- uses clear images
- has information presented in a multisensory way.

To evaluate software for dyslexic learners, ask yourself the following questions:

- Is the design cluttered?
- Does it irritate?
- Does it have voice output?
- How does it motivate, reward success and/or entertain?
- Is it age specific in design?
- Does it address more than one way of learning?
- Can the learner use it independently?
- Does it have a record-keeping system?
- Can the program be individualized?
- Does it include assessment and/or diagnostic features?

Telling the time can be a challenging activity for dyslexic pupils. Clock faces can be complicated because they contain a variety of information.

One idea is to make two clock faces out of cardboard – one has a long minute-hand and dashes for minutes around the edge, the other has a short hour-hand with the numbers 1–12 around its edge. This separates the numbers from the minute-hand. Emphasize that the minute-hand is long and equate it with the word minute, which is also long. The minute-hand goes around the clock quite quickly. The second clock face has a short hour-hand emphasizing that the word hour is short. The hour-hand moves slowly around the clock.

A number of games and activities can be introduced using the two clock faces, but the idea is to get the pupil to recognize the different characteristics between the hour-hand and its function and the minute-hand and its function.

It may be helpful to provide the children with two blank clock faces and let them fill in the minutes and the hours. This will be more explicit and help to secure the concepts of minutes and hours. Then consolidate by putting the hours and minutes together. If penmanship is a concern, use stickers or glue for the numbers as opposed to writing them in.

TWO CLOCK FACES

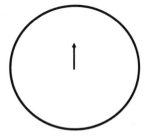

Getting children to sing their times tables can be a fun activity and young children in particular react well to this. It also takes away a lot of the anxieties associated with rote memory experienced by dyslexic children. You can make a tape of songs for each of the tables and the children will quickly learn them. It can even form a good introduction to the lesson and can be on when the children arrive and leave the class to encourage them to sing along.

Worksheets can also be developed to accompany the tape, with spaces for the children to fill in the missing letters or numbers. For example, use songs with words such as, 'Two little caterpillars crawling on the floor, they were joined by two more then there were four. Four little caterpillars looking for the door and then they were joined by another two more.' Ask the children how many are there now. Add drawings of caterpillars to the worksheet.

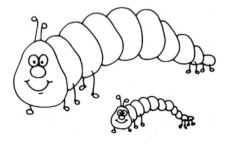

It is important to encourage children with dyslexia to develop their own strategies. In mathematics this can be related to their own learning styles – for example, the inchworm and the grasshopper. The inchworm prefers small pieces of information and a step-by-step approach while the grasshopper prefers a more holistic and global way of working and may omit several steps in the problem-solving process. It is important to discuss different styles with the child and try to work out together what might be best suited for him. Learner independence is important and this can be achieved through learner choice, decision making, type of learning activities and encouraging students to become more aware of the learning process they are embarking on. This is particularly important for children with dyslexia. Developing their own strategy plan such as the one below may be helpful.

My strategy plan for mathematics		
Activity	**Things that help**	**Things to avoid**
Times tables		
Understanding questions		
Remembering formulae		
Organizing		
Remembering symbols		
Remembering homework		
Maths vocabulary		
Difficulty reading charts, graphs and diagrams		
Remaining calm when doing maths		

Each of the above points can be discussed with the pupil and his responses should be noted and then discussed again to ensure that he can use the strategy effectively.

DEVELOPING OWN STRATEGIES

Dyslexia across the curriculum

Provide opportunities for dyslexic pupils to talk extensively in the history classroom. This can allow them to engage in 'print-free' debate and utilize their strengths in oral discussion. Talking through an issue also helps the pupils to develop a theme in sequence, and practice in discussion will improve the pupils' abilities to question, infer, deduce, propose and evaluate. For example, a topic on the origins of World War Two might involve the following:

- Question – why did the war break out?
- Infer – to what extent was World War One responsible?
- Deduce – what was the motive for each of the countries for joining in with the war?
- Propose – 'I propose the Treaty of Versailles was responsible for the outbreak of World War Two.'
- Evaluate – who were the real victors at the end of the war? What was the real cost of the war?

A good history exercise which is effective in generating talk is to do a group investigation of photographs of typical families between 1880 and 1960. This requires pupils to pool their collective knowledge of social history in order to identify the key features of the families' backgrounds. Exercises of this kind utilize the latent historical knowledge of pupils who may be visually literate and articulate, yet reticent to transfer their knowledge into written form. This exercise provokes a great deal of discussion and encourages pupils to generate their own elaborate theories.

TALK, TALK, TALK

These activities are particularly effective for dyslexic learners because they involve the pupil almost immediately in active decision-making and problem-solving processes.

Card-matching games can be used to engage reluctant readers with substantial amounts of information, acting as an alternative to teacher-led lessons. Groups are given a set of cards bearing key information about a novel, such as the characters and the plot and required to match this information to another set of information, such as a description of a character or a location of a scene. Participants have to draw on their collective recall and understanding of the novel. The cards can be structured so as to encourage pupils to draw appropriate inferences and conclusions from the novel. This exercise can be used to establish the basic sequence of the novel and can provide a helpful reference point or memory trigger for dyslexic pupils in subsequent lessons.

Games can also be designed to enhance a dyslexic pupil's familiarity with key vocabulary and concepts from a given topic. For example, a simple board game can replicate the discipline, financial hardship and physical pain suffered by poor people working in a textile factory during the period of a Dickens novel. The pupils begin the week with a full wage and a full set of limbs displayed upon graphic cards. Landing on chance square requires the pupil to read out his fate and surrender cash and/or relinquish a limb.

Pupils are given the constituent sentences of an essay printed on separate strips of paper and are required to reconstruct the whole. This is a particularly useful exercise for helping weaker writers develop an appreciation of how successful paragraphs are constructed and how different kinds of paragraphs, such as introductions and conclusions, have different functions within a piece of writing. Presented as a puzzle, it helps solve the motivational difficulties, which dyslexic pupils can frequently present when required to undertake critical textual analysis. This can lead on to the following activities:

- displaying appropriate paragraph and sentence stems and similar prompts and cues on the classroom wall or board
- organizing peer help in planning and drafting different kinds of written work
- providing support to alert pupils to possible difficulties when introducing them to unfamiliar writing styles such as academic, journalistic, bureaucratic, reminiscent
- setting clear, high expectations of technical accuracy with regards to structure, grammar, punctuation and spelling in finished work, while providing support by explaining demands precisely and planning in sufficient time for drafting and amendment processes.

Diagrams can be used across the curriculum for children with dyslexia. Information organized in a diagram can be referred to easily and can often enable an ease of understanding children don't get from reading text. Diagrams should encapsulate the key points by using only key words and phrases rather than large amounts of text often seen in children's notes. This will enable the child to see, absorb and understand the information more effectively and in a shorter amount of time. Ideally, the child should build or draw and label the diagram themselves. This type of experiential learning can be very useful in linking concepts and consolidating learning.

Diagrams can be used for brainstorming and writing but are also very useful for note-taking and will be especially helpful to study from. Children could also be encouraged, when taking notes, to construct a flow diagram in their note-taking using indents, shapes, colours and arrows. For example, headings can be inside rectangles, subheadings slightly indented and underlined and then the key points indented further and in bullet form. When one event leads into another, add an arrow, connecting the two together. Children could also insert drawings that are relevant and meaningful to what they are learning. Children's diagrams need not be masterpieces. They should be encouraged to keep them plain and simple with a lot of white space for readability. When students go back to study from a flow diagram, the placement of the words on the paper will show relationships and draw their eyes to the relevant information. For example, they will know that all the headings will be in rectangles so if they are looking for something specific, it can be more easily found.

One final point regarding labelling and constructing diagrams is in a test situation. Be sure the child is familiar with the diagram you are asking them to label. For example, if you are asking them to label a diagram of the planets in our solar system, give them the same diagram in a test situation as the one they have been studying from. To give them a different one could completely disorient their thinking and result in confusion and failure when in fact they were prepared and feeling confident in their knowledge.

LABELLING AND CONSTRUCTING DIAGRAMS

GENERALIZING CONCEPTS

Pupils with dyslexia can have a difficulty in generalizing scientific concepts as many of the concepts occur across different branches of science. For example, ecosystem, respiration and homeostasis are all abstract concepts and it can be difficult for the dyslexic pupil to recognize that the same concept can apply to other areas of science.

Construct a chart and along the left-hand column insert each of the concepts that are relevant to the pupil's current studies in science. In the next column insert some key words relating to the concept that is being learnt. For example, if the concept is respiration, key words could be 'breathing', the 'respiratory cycle', 'oxygen', and so on. In the next column get the pupil to give specific examples of how these can apply to different areas of science – for example, the respiratory system in mammals and fish. The idea is to generalize the concept of respiration across the spectrum of science, including animals and plants.

Some ideas that can help make modern foreign languages more dyslexia friendly include the following:

- Get the pupils involved in the culture of the country. Have a food day when they take pictures of and taste examples of food from different countries and regions.
- Add mime and gesture to words to emphasize the accent of the language.
- Add pictures to text – use pictures from the country of the language being studied.
- Use colour to highlight gender, accents.
- Use games to consolidate vocabulary – make packs of pocket-sized cards and get the pupils to say the word each time they see a card.
- Combine listening and reading by providing text and tape. This is particularly useful for dyslexic pupils as they often need to see and hear the word.
- Allow a pupil to produce his own tape of himself speaking the language.
- Stimulate interest in the country by showing films, reading poems and discussing famous people from that country.
- Provide rules and other information about the language in written form for further study and future reference.

MAKING LANGUAGES DYSLEXIA FRIENDLY

IMPROVISATION

One of the best ways to start off a drama group is to introduce some basic improvisation. This can be done in the form of a game such as charades or statues. The teacher can lead the way by asking the group to guess what the actors are doing. Keep it simple and easy, acting out scenes like window cleaning or a policeman on traffic duty. The key to success is maintaining the pupils' enthusiasm.

Some improvisations can be produced from a basic starting point – for example, a short piece may be devised by the pupils working in pairs, based on something of their choice. This can make it meaningful to them and the quality of the improvisation will be enhanced because of this. This is really important for dyslexic pupils because they may be self-conscious of performing in front of the class, but an improvisation that involves fun and mime will be less threatening for them.

One good way of getting the improvisation started is to produce a photograph – something that can arouse emotions – and have a discussion before the pupils begin.

Other starting points may be an object or group of objects – pupils can choose from a selection, and some exciting, often hilarious, outcomes can result. This approach takes much of the strain away from reading, traditionally associated with drama studies, and helps to build enthusiasm for the subject.

In music, dyslexic pupils can be faced with many challenges – even if they have a good ear. Most of their difficulties arise from reading musical scores. Visual discrimination can be a problem, for example, when two clefs have subtle differences. Unstable vision can result in the apparent movement of lines and spaces, omissions and insertions.

To make reading music dyslexia friendly use large stave music by enlarging a normal sized score. A colour overlay may also help to reduce visual discomfort, or use tinted paper. Mnemonics can also be used to reduce the need to read every note – for example, in the treble clef: Every Good Boy Deserves Favour, and in the bass clef: Great Big Dogs From Africa. It is also an idea to remove any unnecessary information from the score, such as repeated rhythms or melodies. The aim is to make the score as uncluttered as possible for the dyslexic pupil by removing any notes that do not pertain to the instrument he is playing – certainly to begin with. These can always be added later, once the pupil has mastered the piece.

Develop a dyslexia-friendly checklist for the school and for colleagues who may know less about dyslexia. The checklist could include the following:

- Is the teaching multisensory?
- Is the pace of work differentiated?
- Is the assessment of learning outcomes varied?
- Is the dyslexic pupil's learning style being taken into account?
- Are you including study/memory skills in the daily classroom activities?
- Are the worksheets in large type and well spaced, with visuals and short sentences?
- Is non-white paper being used?
- Is the layout of the desks helpful in terms of concentration and does it minimize distractions?
- Are pupils being encouraged to present their work using a word processor?
- Are lessons well planned to take account of the dyslexic learner? For example, does each lesson begin with an overview?
- Is the lesson broken up to minimize fatigue?
- Are oral instructions kept short?
- Are there opportunities for pupils to reflect on their learning?
- Is the environment in the classroom as stress free as possible?
- Are all staff proactive in promoting dyslexia-friendly materials and teaching?
- Is there whole-school awareness training in dyslexia?

Examinations can be very challenging for students with dyslexia and often they may not perform to their full potential in exams. This can be due to a number of different factors including examination stress and misreading the question as well as ineffective revision technique. This latter point is very important as this is where they will need specific guidance as revision can be time consuming and it is important that the student uses his time efficiently.

Children will have their own learning style and in order to revise effectively they should consider what works best for them. Have them create a study plan by first asking themselves how they learn best.

By creating visual images?

> Create drawings, pictures or diagrams. Highlight text or simply create a mental visual image. Mind-maps may also be helpful.

By reading, note-taking and copying?

> Create index cards with key points on the front and supporting information on the back.

By repeating information?

> Study with a partner by reading important information aloud and then explaining it in your own words.

Other pointers that can be discussed are:

- ✓ Never try to memorize something you don't understand. Try to learn it and then explain it in your own words.
- ✓ Look at titles, headings and subheadings. Ask yourself why it is significant and what key points can be listed under each heading.
- ✓ Create question and answer cards.
- ✓ Create tape recordings to listen to.

- ✓ Try to connect it to something you already know.
- ✓ Create a mnemonic to help remember key points, vocabulary or sequences.
- ✓ Time: plan to study in smaller, frequent increments rather than sitting down for a long period. Do not try to fit it all into one night.
- ✓ Take regular breaks to get up, stretch, move around and get fresh air.
- ✓ Drink plenty of water.
- ✓ Choose a location that is good for working. Be honest about how much noise and interruption you will have. Being in front of the television, texting and an open facebook page on your computer or phone are not going to allow you to be completely focused.
- ✓ Create a revision timetable. Be realistic and stick to it.

The common view is that children with dyslexia often find change quite difficult and particularly the transition to secondary school. It is natural for children to experience anxiety around transitions as they move from a place they feel safe to a place that is unknown. Therefore, it is important that this transfer is well planned and the student is gradually introduced to the new school. Most schools will have an established programme where all new students visit the high school late in the summer term for a half day. They have a tour of the school and meet the teachers. While they do experience the vastness of the building, they are often the only ones there so they don't experience the crush of students in the corridors. It is a good idea to have leadership students available for the first week of school to walk students through their class schedule, showing them where each class is, where their locker is and how to plan what they will take with them as well as their route through the school. These students could also be available to check in with them at various points throughout the day for the first week or two. Most students with dyslexia may need the additional support offered by transition groups but the important point is that they will not be singled out and will be receiving the same kind of support as the rest of the students.

Have the child create a chart with issues they are concerned about on one side and how they will feel prepared on the other. An example of possible concerns is provided below:

Concerns	What will make me feel supported?
School building • Finding classes • Eating lunch • Finding the toilets • Vastness of the building	
Developing friendship groups • How do I find my friends between classes and at lunch	
Timetable • Getting to my next class • Remembering what classes are when • What to take with you each day	
Subjects/curriculum • Support if I don't understand – will the teachers know me and know about dyslexia • Friends seeing me visit the counsellors • Managing homework • Level of difficulty • Pace of work	
Lockers • Finding my locker • When do I go to my locker • Opening the lock • Who has the locker next to mine • Where will my friends be	

This can also be a daunting prospect for students with dyslexia. There are high expectations at college and there will be other students there who will seem to pass exams with ease and this can be quite intimidating for students with dyslexia. They may start to doubt their own abilities. It is important therefore that they get off to a good start at college and do not experience initial hurdles which may undermine their confidence.

It is a good idea to develop a checklist of areas that the student will need to consider.

GENERAL QUESTIONS

General questions	Response
What type of course am I suited to?	
Are there any courses I should avoid?	
Will I be supported at college or university? Should I declare my dyslexia in my application forms?	
How can I develop strategies to deal with dyslexia?	

Areas that need support	Response
Lectures, lecture notes and seminars	
Practical sessions	
Field trips	
Study skills	
Using libraries, learning centres and information centres	

You can add points to this checklist as you go along but it is important to keep a record of this and share it with the student. Eventually you can get the student to develop his own checklist using the areas covered in the one above.

Often children and adults with dyslexia can achieve to a high level but they fail to acknowledge this. It is too easy for someone who experiences challenges in an area of learning to feel a lack of success even if that is not actually the case. If one has experienced failure in the learning situation it is difficult to reverse this even though it may only be one's perception of failure and in fact they may not have failed at all. Perceptions though can be very strong and it can be difficult to shift this once the negative perceptions have become ingrained.

You can get the student to develop a personal learning progress chart for himself. This should provide a clear view of what the student has achieved and what has still to be accomplished.

My personal learning progress			
Subject	**What I have done**	**What I need to do**	**How to do this**
English	Read the novel for our novel study	Read the critical reviews on the novel	Start with a peer group discussion of the novel
History	Described the causes of World War Two	Look at the causes in more detail	Watch the DVD of the news archives available in the library
Biology	Labelled the different areas of the body	Describe each of the parts in more detail	Use a mind-map
Mathematics	Understood the new formulae that has been provided for algebra	Do some practical examples using this formulae	Obtain a revision book showing examples and answers for self-correction
Physical education	Identified the different muscles involved in playing basketball	Show how these muscles are used in other sports and activities	Watch DVD on exercise and sport

This type of chart can help to provide the learner with dyslexia a sense of ownership over his learning and also a realistic view of what they have actually achieved. This column is more important than what they have still to achieve. One of the most effective ways of reinforcing this is thorough feedback. Positive feedback is important for children and all young people with dyslexia – the feedback needs to be appropriate, positive and realistic as well as specific.

Help them all recognize and enjoy their successes!

GLOSSARY

ADHD – children with ADHD (attention difficulties with hyperactivity) will have a short attention span and tend to work on a number of different tasks at the same time. They will be easily distracted and may have difficulty settling in some classrooms, particularly if there is a number of competing distractions. It is also possible for some children to have attention difficulties without hyperactivity. (This is referred to as ADD.)

Auditory discrimination – many children with dyslexia can have difficulties with auditory discrimination. It refers to the difficulties in identifying specific sounds and in distinguishing these sounds with other similar sounds. This can be associated with the phonological difficulties experienced by children with dyslexia (see phonological difficulties). Hearing loss or partial and intermittent hearing loss can also be associated with auditory discrimination.

Bottom-up – this refers to the method of reading using decoding skills therefore reading accuracy is crucial. It means that the reader has to have a good grasp of the letters and the sounds and be able to blend these together to make words. Some readers with dyslexia confuse words with similar sounds or those that look visually similar. It is common for beginning readers to learn to read this way. It is essential that children with dyslexia are taught through the bottom-up process in order to ensure they can be familiar with the basic sounds and sound combinations (for comparison see top-down method).

Cognitive – this refers to the learning and thinking process. It is the process that describes how learners take in information and how they retain and understand the information.

Decoding – this refers to the reading processing and specifically to the breaking down of words into the individual sounds.

Differentiation – this is the process of adapting materials and teaching to suit a range of learners abilities and level of attainments. Usually differentiation refers to the task, the teaching, the resources and the assessment. Each of these areas can be differentiated to suit the needs of individual or groups of learners.

Dyscalculia – this describes children and adults who have difficulties in numeracy. This could be due to difficulties in computation of numbers, remembering numbers or reading the instructions associated with number problems.

Dysgraphia – this is difficulties in handwriting. Some dyspraxic and dyslexic children may also show signs of dysgraphia. Children with dysgraphia will benefit from lined paper as they have visual/spatial problems and they may have an awkward pencil grip.

Dyslexia – refers to difficulties in accessing print but also other factors such as memory, processing speed, sequencing, directions, syntax, spelling and written work can also be challenging. Children with dyslexia often have phonological difficulties which results in poor word attack skills. In many cases they require a dedicated one-to-one intervention programme.

Dyslexia friendly – refers to the complete learning experience of the child. This includes how materials are presented, how the student is taught and assessed and the degree of awareness of dyslexia among teaching staff and management.

Dyspraxia – this refers to children and adults with coordination difficulties. It can also be described as Developmental Coordination Disorder (DCD).

Emotional literacy – this refers to the extent to which children are aware of their emotions and feelings and particularly those of others.

Eye tracking – this is the skill of being able to read a line and keep the eyes on track throughout the line. Children with poor eye tracking may omit lines or words on a page. Sometimes masking a part of a line or page, or using a ruler can help with eye tracking.

Information processing – this is a process that describes how children and adults learn new information. It is usually described as a cycle – input, cognition and output. Often children with dyslexia can have difficulties at all the stages of information processing and dyslexia can be referred to a difficulty or a difference in information processing.

Kinaesthetic memory – this refers to the memory used for movement such as remembering exercise routines. Learning handwriting is an example of how young utilize their kinaesthetic memory.

Learned helplessness – this refers to the cycle of failure that some children may experience particularly if they have repeated failures at the same task. The extent of this failure is reinforced by subsequent failures and it becomes a learnt response to a task. Many children with dyslexia can experience learned helplessness with reading as they have repeated failures when engaged in this type of activity.

Learning disabilities – this is a general term to describe the range of specific learning difficulties such as dyslexia, dyspraxia, dyscalculia and dysgraphia. Often referred to as LD it is not equated with intelligence and children with LD are usually in the average to above average intelligence range.

Learning styles – this can describe the learners preferences for learning – this can be using visual, auditory, kinaesthetic or tactile stimuli but it can also relate to environmental preferences such as sound, the use of music when learning, preferences for time of day and working in pairs, groups or individually. There is a lot of literature on learning styles but it is still seen as quite controversial very likely because there are hundreds of different instruments all of which claim to measure learning styles and many learners are in fact quite adaptable and can adapt to different types of learning situations and environments. Nevertheless it is a useful concept to apply in the classroom, particularly for children with learning disabilities as using learning styles it is more possible to identify their strengths and use these in preparing materials and in teaching.

Long-term memory – this is used to recall information that has been learnt and needs to be recalled for a purpose. Many children with dyslexia can have difficulty with long-term memory as they have not organized the information they have learnt and recalling it can be challenging as they may not have enough cues to assist with recall. Study skills programmes can help with long-term memory.

Metacognition – this is the process of thinking about thinking – that is being aware of how one learns and how a problem was solved. It is a process-focused approach and one that is necessary for effective and efficient learning. Many children with dyslexia may have poor metacognitive awareness because they are unsure of the process of learning. For that reason study skills programmes can be useful.

Multiple intelligence – first developed by Howard Gardner in the early 1980s in his book *Frames of Mind* it turns conventional views of intelligence on its head. Gardner provides insights into eight intelligences and shows how the educational and the social and emotional needs of all children can be catered for through the use of these intelligences. Traditionally, intelligence has been equated with school success but often this focuses predominantly on the verbal and language aspects of performance. Gardner broadens this view and indicates that the traditional view of intelligence can be unnecessarily restrictive and misleading.

Multisensory – this refers to the use of a range of modalities in learning. In this context multisensory usually refers to the use of visual, auditory, kinaesthetic and tactile learning. It is generally accepted that children with dyslexia need a multisensory approach that utilizes all of these modalities.

Neurological – this refers to brain associated factors – this could be brain structure – that is the different components of the brain or brain processing how the components interact with each other. The research in dyslexia shows that both brain structure and brain processing factors are implicated in dyslexia.

Paired reading – this involves the child and the tutor (or parent) reading aloud at the same time.

Peer tutoring – this is when two or more children work together and try to learn from each other. It may also be the case that an older more proficient learner is working with a younger less accomplished learner and the younger one is the tutee and the older the tutor.

Phonological awareness – this refers to the processing of becoming familiar with the letter sounds and letter combinations that make the sounds in reading print. There are 44 sounds in the English language and some sounds are very similar in sounding. This can be confusing and challenging for children with dyslexia and they often get the sounds confused or have difficulty in retaining and recognizing them when reading or in speech.

Reciprocal reading – the aim is to encourage the child to check his own comprehension. Small units of text are presented and the tutor reads aloud first and summarizes what has been read. The purpose is for the tutor to model the read-aloud and think-aloud process and to encourage the child to self-question to actively obtain meaning from the text.

Scanning – this refers to the process involved when one is attempting to locate a particular word or piece of information on a page.

Skimming – refers to the process of reading by focusing on the key words only.

Shared reading – the child and the tutor (or parent) take turns in reading. The aim is to extend the language experience of the child.

Specific Learning Difficulties (SpLD) – this refers to the range of difficulties experienced in general that can be of a specific nature such as reading, coordination, spelling, handwriting. There are quite a number of specific learning difficulties and they can be seen as being distinct from general learning difficulties. In the latter case children with general learning difficulties usually find most areas of the curriculum challenging and may have a lower level of comprehension than children with specific learning difficulties.

TextHelp® – commercially available software to help with spelling, writing and reading comprehension – new versions have many additional features and is suitable for both children and adults.

Top-down – this refers to the reading process and particularly the procedure and strategies used by young readers. The top-down method means that the reader begins with the context and the background of the text and uses contextual cues to help with the reading process. In the top-down model, reading for meaning is more important than reading accuracy. Language experience is an important prerequisite for reading using the top-down method (see bottom-up method for comparison).

Overlearning – this refers to repeating the same task, or piece of learning, a number of times to help the learner consolidate the information.

Working memory – this is the first stage in short-term memory. It involves holding information in short-term store and carrying out a processing activity simultaneously. This can be solving a problem, reading instructions or merely walking around. Working memory is when one or more stimuli is held in memory for a short period of time. Children with dyslexia often experience difficulties with working memory as they have difficulty in holding a number of different pieces of information at the same time.

WEBSITES

http://dyslexiaassociation.org.au
www.arkellcentre.org.uk
www.barringtonstoke.co.uk
www.bda-dyslexia.org.uk
www.crossboweducation.com
www.das.org.sg
www.donjohnston.co.uk
www.drgavinreid.com
www.dyslexia.eu.com
www.dyslexia-international.org
www.dyslexiafoundation.org.nz
www.dyslexiascotland.org.uk
www.dyslexic.com
www.funtrack.com.au
www.globaleducationalconsultants.com
www.helpingchildrenwithdyslexia.com
www.icepe.ie
www.interdys.org
www.ldonline.com
www.learning-works.org.uk
www.lighthouseschoolonline.com
www.ogtutors.com
www.redroseschool.co.uk
www.speld.org.nz
www.speld-sa.org.au
www.texthelp.com
www.worldofdyslexia.com